Beginner's Guide to Hydroponics

SOILLESS GARDENING

Beginner's Guide to Hydroponics
SOILLESS GARDENING

by James Sholto Douglas
CONSULTING MEMBER, INTERNATIONAL
WORKING-GROUP ON SOILLESS CULTURE
[IWOSC]

General Publishing Company Limited
Don Mills, Ontario

Published in Canada 1976 by
General Publishing Company Limited
30 Lesmill Road
Don Mills, Ontario

ISBN 0-7736-1020-0

Printed in U.S.A.

Contents

FIGURES

ACKNOWLEDGEMENTS

The author is indebted to the following institutions for permission to reproduce photographs and wishes to record his thanks for their interest and support: 1 and 4, Publicity Department, Government of West Bengal; 3, University of Florida; 5, Hydroponic Investigation Unit, Sibpur; 11, British Mushroom Growers Association; 14, Agricultural Research Service of the United States of America; 16, University of Florida; 17, Hydroponics, Inc.

The other photographs were taken by the author.

Beginner's Guide to Hydroponics

SOILLESS GARDENING

Preface

There are many amateur gardeners and householders who would like to take up hydroponics if only they knew how to set about it. Others may be equally anxious to begin growing plants without soil but perhaps feel some diffidence in starting off on a new system in the absence of clear and well defined guidance. Possibly they have heard, or been told—quite inaccurately as it happens—that soilless gardening is rather complicated and requires special knowledge. This idea that hydroponics *always* needs a very high standard of technical ability to make it succeed has discouraged large numbers of people from even trying it out. In fact, whatever the case in the past was, there is, in existence today, at least cne extremely simple method of gardening without soil that can be used with complete confidence by ordinary gardeners, housewives and indeed anyone prepared to follow a few basic and easily understood rules. Those people who have started simplified hydroponics have been delighted with the results that they have obtained and the excellent quality of the flowers and vegetables that they have grown so successfully in such short periods of time, without any particular effort or expense.

So why not you? This book details a really simple way of growing your household supplies of garden flowers and greenfood. No soil at all is required. The beginner is introduced, step by step, to hydroponics and shown how to set up and operate easy-to-use soilless gardens in the home or backyard. The method recommended has been tested by long experience and found to be well suited to the needs cf amateurs and housewives. Clear and concise instructions are given about daily work and the care of hydroponic units.

In writing this book I have endeavoured to put myself in the place of the newcomer to soilless gardening. It has always been obvious to me—as indeed it is to many other workers in the field of horticulture—that hydroponics cannot fulfil its true purpose until its advantages have been put fully at the disposal of all interested people. The chief object in devising a really simple method of growing plants without soil is to ensure that anyone who wishes to use hydroponics in his or her home may not be denied the chance to do so by lack of access to the necessary information.

Hydroponics can be an enjoyable hobby, a profitable pastime or a way of adding to your income by growing your own fresh produce at home. It will also lead you towards a better understanding of Nature and a deeper knowledge of biological science. Gardening is dear to the hearts of most of us and in soilless culture you will surely find the means to keep in close and regular contact with plant life. Added to all this is the fact that hydroponics demands no hard work or long hours of labour.

Begin with the simple method recommended in this book. Once you have become familiar with it, branch out, if you wish, into some of the more advanced techniques discussed in the final chapter. But no matter how small your soilless garden may be—or remain— you will always find something to delight you in the ease and simplicity of amateur hydroponics.

J. SHOLTO DOUGLAS

CHAPTER I

The Facts about Hydroponics

Hydroponics is generally defined in modern encyclopedias and dictionaries as the science of growing plants without using soil by feeding them on solutions of water and mineral salts, instead of relying upon the traditional methods of cultivating the earth which most gardeners and farmers still continue to do in order to raise crops. However, because such a description could sound a little complicated let us begin by thinking in simpler terms.

It is not always realised that hydroponics may be employed in numerous ways, ranging from the large-scale production of commercial foodstuffs—flowers and fruits, through medium-sized office and community growing units, right down to smaller lots of colourful home blooms and indoor plants, or tasty vegetables and succulent salads for the household, or as a family hobby. This striking versatility of soilless culture, combined with the excellent results that can be obtained in all kinds of places, has made the system ideal for widely differing conditions. In fact, hydroponic gardening can be easier and more pleasant to do than ordinary soil gardening. During the past few years an immense amount of scientific research has been undertaken to develop really simple and practical ways of growing plants without soil; methods which can be used confidently by amateurs and housewives. So do not be put off by something you have perhaps read about hydroponics being a complicated procedure requiring special skills or knowledge for success. On the contrary, simplified gardening without soil is basically straightforward, if you follow the few easy rules. Naturally, in big commercial units there has to be technical control, but for growing plants in the home or ordinary garden, backyard or window ledge, what matter most are love, care, and ability to stick to the guidelines laid down.

MEANING AND PURPOSE

The term hydroponics is derived from two Greek words, *hudor*, water, and *ponos*, work. When combined, these mean 'water-working'—and a reference to the use of solutions of water and fertiliser chemicals for soilless plant cultivation, as opposed to normal growth in soil or geoponics (the care of the earth). Quite a number of different methods of hydroponics are today in general usage throughout the world, the exact choice depending upon local needs and conditions. However, they all conform to the same basic principles and all have one common objective—the growing of plants quite independently of earth or organic matter. This capacity for divorcing the cultivation of flowers, vegetables, fruits and grains from the soil has profound implications for the development of horticulture and farming. In short, it means that mankind is no longer solely dependent on the land for sustenance and the satisfaction of natural desires for a beautiful environment, because gardeners and farmers can now produce lovely flowers and raise fine crops without any soil in almost any place they may wish.

Given a minimum supply of water, hydroponic units, both small and large, may be set up in towns and cities, for the enjoyment and use of urban populations, while people living in deserts or barren regions can raise quantities of attractive and healthy plants even under the very infertile conditions common in such areas.

Apart from these general considerations hydroponics also offers certain important advantages to the individual gardener or householder, including better quality plants, quicker growth, much saving of time and labour (with the elimination of troublesome tasks like digging, weeding and manuring), lower costs, complete absence of dirt and smells, extremely consistent results and year-round attractive displays of blooms or quantities of fresh greenstuff in the home.

The new simple methods, which are described in this book, make it possible for anyone to raise first-class plants without difficulty, even in the most congested surroundings. Housewives, flat and apartment dwellers, backyard or window-box gardeners, or those possessing roof space, indeed amateurs of every type, in any land, can now use hydroponics to brighten up their daily lives.

HOW IT BEGAN

The story of the discovery and development of gardening without soil is quite a fascinating one. It all began nearly three centuries ago when John Woodward, a Fellow of the Royal Society of England, started experiments to try to find out how plants obtained their food supplies. Using water cultures, Woodward attempted to determine whether it was the water or the solid particles of soil that nourished crops. Handicapped by lack of proper equipment, however, he could make little progress nor could other scientists who followed him, until the beginning of the Nineteenth Century, when research methods were revolutionised by advances made in the field of chemistry. These enabled compounds to be split up into their constituent parts, so that at last it became possible to draw up a tentative list of the nutrients used by plants. In 1804, Nicolas de Saussure published some results of investigations he had made that showed how plants needed mineral substances to achieve satisfactory growth. Later, Jean Boussingault, a French scientist, was able to raise crops in pots full of sand and charcoal to which chemical solutions of known composition were added. During the years 1859–65, Julius Von Sachs, Professor of Botany at the University of Würzburg, in Germany, conducted further trials which made possible the development of a laboratory type of soilless culture. By adding balanced proportions of fertiliser chemicals to water, Von Sachs found that he could grow plants in the absence of any earth or manures under carefully controlled conditions. Soon, many scientists studying plant nutrition in various countries began to employ this novel technique in their laboratories for experimental purposes. By 1920, it had been accepted universally for such work.

It was not until about ten years later, however, in 1929–30, that an American professor, Dr William F. Gericke, of the University of California, attempted to transform laboratory-style soilless cultivation into practical crop growing without soil. Reasoning that if it could become possible to produce plants where ordinary earth or manures could not be used, or where soil gardening would be out of the question, something of real and lasting value to humanity would have been achieved, Gericke set up out-of-door growing units, taking advantage of the sunny Californian climate. His trials were brilliantly successful, so much so that his soilless cultured tomato crops attained heights of over twenty-five feet and picking of the fruits had to be done with the aid of ladders. Naming the new garden science 'hydroponics', he then went on to raise a wide variety of other vegetables, as well as flowers, grains, root crops and fruits.

With the publication of the results of these Californian tests, the use of hydroponics spread rapidly across the United States. Many university departments and scientific institutions started trial units, while commercial growers and nurserymen began to appreciate the advantages of soilless gardening. In Europe, too, the novel system attracted considerable attention in knowledgeable horticultural and farming circles. The University of Reading, famous for its pioneering work in new cropping techniques, as well as the internationally important firm of Imperial Chemical Industries Ltd., undertook the adaptation of hydroponics to British conditions.

Following the outbreak of world war in 1939, soilless gardening received a further impetus. Both the American Army and the Royal Air Force opened hydroponic units at military bases. Many millions of tons of vegetables produced without soil were eaten by Allied soldiers and airmen during the war years. As hydroponics became more widely used in different regions, numerous changes and alternative methods appeared, all developed from the original system. Nevertheless, most of these were rather complicated and generally needed expert attention. To overcome such difficulties, the author, in collaboration with the Government of West Bengal, opened a hydroponic centre at the Experimental Station near Darjeeling, in India, in 1946, with the object of evolving a really simple and inexpensive method of soilless gardening suitable for use by any ordinary person without special training. So successful were the results obtained that within a comparatively short period of time it was possible to extend simplified hydroponics to other countries. In fact, the work started at Darjeeling, combined with the researches of other scientists and the practical experiences of countless growers and interested technical institutions, as well as commercial firms, forms the basis of the easy-to-use method of soilless gardening described for beginners in this book.

CURRENT USAGE

Not many years ago, if you did not know what it meant, you

would have found it quite difficult to look up the word hydroponics. Today, however, there is hardly any standard work of reference that does not list the soilless culture of plants. In itself, this is a good measure of the progress of the science and art of hydroponics. There is now no continent in the world where hydroponic gardens and farms are not flourishing and few lands which lack any knowledge of one or other of the various methods of plant growth without soil. Big commercial units in north America and Europe, as well as in Japan, turn out quantities of fresh produce all the year around to feed landless city dwellers. In the Sahara desert and the sandy wastes of the Arabian peninsula, oil companies maintain hydroponic installations to supply their employees with health-giving greenfood. The American Armed Forces still operate their soilless gardens in the Far East, while in India thousands of householders raise essential vegetables in simple hydroponic units on rooftops or in backyards. Countries like the Canary Islands balance their economies by exporting vast amounts of soilless-produced tomatoes, cucumbers and salads to industrial states like Britain every year. From the Caribbean area, too, Puerto Rican and Mexican growers ship immense quantities of luscious hydroponic fruits and greenstuff to the insatiable United States and Canadian markets. In England, Germany, France, the Netherlands and Switzerland, flower firms often prefer to employ the soilless method for commercial purposes, especially for the production of carnations and other quality blooms. Roses and chrysanthemums are grown extensively in Colorado and neighbouring states for export and last year nurseries in those areas made gross profits of over ten million pounds (£1 sterling = $2·41 in 1971) from hydroponically raised flowers alone.

The authorities in the U.S.S.R., have encouraged the extension of hydroponics. Large hothouse, soilless farms and gardens exist at Moscow and Kiev, while in Armenia an Institute of Hydroponics has been established at Erevan in the Caucasus region. Officially, soilless cultivation of plants is looked upon in Russia as a biological industry coming in between horticulture and manufacturing. Other countries, not already mentioned, where hydroponics is in current use include Australia, New Zealand, Spain, South Africa, Israel—particularly in the Negev desert and along the Dead Sea—Italy, the Scandinavian lands, the Bahama Islands, Central and East Africa, Kuwait, Brazil, Poland, the Seychelles, Singapore and Malaya, and

Iran. This list is not, of course, by any means exhaustive, but it does give some idea of how widely spread soilless gardening is today.

Commercially, hydroponics is doing well, but that is not the whole story. Hundreds of thousands of amateur gardeners and housewives throughout the world are also reaping the rewards of taking up soilless culture in their homes. Particularly in urban areas, people feel a real need to have indoor flowers and house plants around them and a source of fresh vegetables for kitchen use. Because hydroponics enables anyone to enjoy the beauty and decorative effects of lovely blooms and greenery in the home, at low cost and without the trouble of using soil and manures, as well as constant supplies of tasty greenfood and fruits, it is becoming increasingly popular amongst town dwellers. Such a development must be a matter of great satisfaction. Not only does it improve the quality of life and raise the standard of any environment, but it adds much to the happiness both of individuals and of society in general. Indeed, the psychological satisfaction of growing your own hydroponic plants can contribute appreciably to health and well-being—it is an occupational therapy in itself.

On the research and extension side, the International Working-Group on Soilless Culture (I.W.O.S.C.), affiliated to the International Society for Horticultural Science, with its headquarters located at the Centre for Plant Physiological Research, Wageningen, in the Netherlands, keeps hydroponicists all over the world in contact with each other, as well as dispensing advice and providing consultants, familiar with local conditions, in many countries.

WORLD-WIDE PARTICIPATION

So when you take up hydroponics, you do, in effect, become part of a great army of enthusiasts and workers spread out through almost every country of the globe. No matter how small your soilless garden may be, even one or two pot plants or a few window boxes, you are still utilising the techniques of international science.

Hydroponics is both a technical activity and an art in the real sense of the word. Indoor flowers and house plants, vegetables, fruits and salads, and out-of-door or greenhouse soilless garden crops all call for good arrangement and proper organisation. Blooms require attractive display. Here is where hydroponics helps, enabling gardening to be carried out in places where it would not normally be possible with soils or organic matter like conventional composts and manures, while at the same time offering ample scope for striking effects, individual ingeniuty, and participation in an up-to-date technology. This book has been written specially to guide and instruct the beginner, as well as to explain how simplified home hydroponics works. If it brings new pleasure and interest into your life then it will have fulfilled its chief purpose.

CHAPTER II

Gardens Without Soil

A soilless garden is actually a miniature world of its own, created by human efforts and kept in being by its scientifically balanced controls, but, none-the-less a healthy and viable concern. In hydroponic units, plants flourish because they receive optimum nutrition, ideal growing conditions and proper attention. No hit-and-miss procedures mar or damage their progress and welfare. Instead, their vital needs are anticipated or catered for. This applies to both small and large installations of every kind. Since gardening without soil, unlike ordinary plant cultivation in earth, is an exact and controlled operation, it will generally give better results, provided due care is taken. For amateurs, in particular, hydroponics is a fascinating hobby, keeping them in contact with scientific developments, while its educational value in teaching children and older students the facts about plant life and growth is unsurpassed.

It has already been mentioned briefly that several methods of hydroponics are in common use. All are based on the same principles, employing solutions of water and fertiliser chemicals for feeding the plants. The chief differences occur in the choice of frames and aggregates or growing media, that is the supports for the roots. All plants raised without soil must have some device or material to hold them upright. In the original water culture method, introduced on a practical scale by Dr Gericke, a wire frame was placed over shallow tanks full of liquid nutrients, the roots of the plants descending through the mesh to feed on the solution below. Because aeration was often a problem in damp or colder climates, scientists later devised sand and gravel cultures. Instead of the wire grids, selected mixtures of these inert materials were placed in the growing containers, giving good support for the plants. As time went on, additional substances such as stone chips, leached cinders, vermiculite, sawdust and pebbles, were also found to be satisfactory. Different methods may suit particular localities and factors of cost and availability of materials will enter into the picture.

The simple method of soilless gardening recommended in this book for beginners to start with is the easiest way known at present to commence the growing of flowers, fruits, vegetables and house plants in the home. Amateur gardeners and householders should find no difficulties in installing this type of hydroponic unit. Its basic principles are of course just the same as those which guide large commercial operators in building and managing their units. But before discussing it in detail, however, let us consider briefly exactly how plants do grow and what are the main essentials for their healthy development. For, as in any other activity, a proper understanding of elementary facts is a real aid to better results in practical work.

HOW PLANTS GROW

Although the cycle of plant life is quite intricate, it can be explained in simple terms. A plant is a sort of natural workshop, each section of which is engaged in the task of changing raw food material into living tissue. To ensure good growth all higher or green plants—and the vast majority of flowers and vegetables belong to this category—require certain essential things including *water, light, air, mineral salts*, and *support for the roots*. Unlike animals and human beings, most plants cannot ingest solid or organic food material, so they are obliged to absorb part of their nourishment from gases in the air and part from solutions of inorganic salts or chemicals and water. These simple substances are transformed by the various departments of the plants into living tissue through the expenditure of energy, obtained from light. Some oxygen is needed for these processes, but a major contribution to growth and development is made by the gas called carbon dioxide, present in the atmosphere. To complete the work, mineral salts in combination with water are absorbed through tiny hairs located on the plants' roots, by the use of a force known as osmosis.

Plants always grow upwards, towards the light. To enable them to stand firmly, a satisfactory support is vital. In soil, the earth provides this, but in hydroponics it is necessary to supply alternative devices or growing media. It is important to choose the right kinds of supports because roots need to breathe just as leaves and stems do. At the same time, there has to be enough moisture around them to prevent them from drying off or dying from lack of water and food-

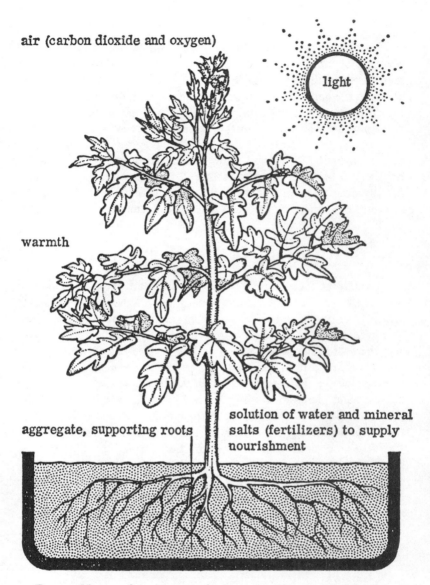

air (carbon dioxide and oxygen)

light

warmth

aggregate, supporting roots

solution of water and mineral salts (fertilizers) to supply nourishment

FIG. 1 How a plant grows in hydroponics. Here we can see how the plant's essential needs are supplied without the use of soil. Nature gives us light, air and water—or we can provide them ourselves, while instead of earth and manures we substitute an aggregate to support the roots and a solution of water and fertiliser salts to furnish adequate foodstuff. Warmth can come from sunshine or different methods of heating.

stuffs. Now, suppose we take a dry seed and watch its behaviour and the different functions of the various parts during development, until it becomes a flowering plant. The easiest way to do this is to bury the seed in a little moist sawdust. Soon, germination will occur and the seed will have absorbed enough water so that the outer skin bursts and the tiny embryo plant which is contained within the seed coat starts to develop. The young root, called the radicle, forces its way downwards to grip firmly the support—in this case the saw-dust—while a small, pointed stem, termed the plumule, grows up-wards towards the light. So far the young plant has developed by feeding on food material stored within the seed and by using the basic essentials that we provided for it—water, air and a support for the roots. Light, too, is present, and available as soon the plumule pushes its way up into the open air, since we have taken care to let sunshine or other illumination reach it daily. But shortly the grow-ing plant will have another demand to make, this time for mineral salts. If these are not supplied the seedling will quickly weaken and die. Consequently, we must feed our plant regularly with some kind of suitable nutrient. If this is done, nothing, except disease or accident, will prevent our seedling from developing into a healthy and mature plant. Here, in easily understandable form, is a com-plete picture of how plants grow and thrive.

THE HYDROPONIC PROCESS

Of the five essential requirements for good plant growing, three are supplied in hydroponics normally by the same means as they are in soil gardening. Water, light, and air are in Nature's gift and may be obtained in the home as part of our surroundings or through the ingenuity of man. But the last two—mineral salts and a support for the roots—must be procured as extras. To cultivate the earth, we dig and hoe and add manures or composts. These latter are organic materials but plants cannot use these directly. They have to go through a lengthy process of weathering or breaking down in the ground before they become available as inorganic nutrients. Even then the gardener or farmer has no real idea of just how much plant food may be present in the land at any given time. In hydroponics, on the other hand, the application of nutrients is a controlled and balanced procedure. It is known that some eleven different elements are, in the main, necessary for good growth, in addition to the oxygen

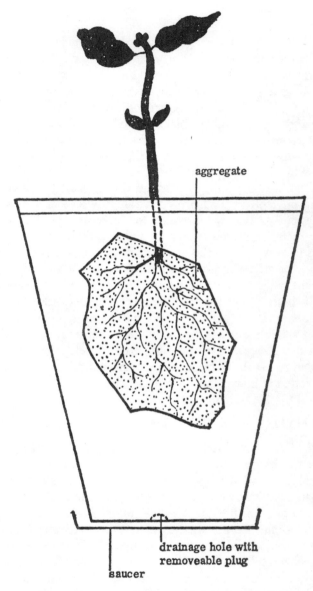

aggregate

drainage hole with
removeable plug

saucer

FIG. 2 Seedling not long after germination in a hydroponic pot.
This diagram shows how the young plant anchors itself in the
growing medium or aggregate, which is kept constantly moist with
the nutrient solution or mixture of water and mineral salts. The
cutaway portion reveals the roots penetrating the aggregate. At the
base of the pot is the drainage hole with removable plug and saucer.

and carbon dioxide supplied from the air. As contained in mineral salts or fertiliser chemicals, these are: *nitrogen, phosphorus, potassium, calcium, magnesium, sulphur, iron, manganese, boron, zinc,* and *copper.* The soilless gardener, therefore, dispenses with the laborious and often back-breaking task of working the land and instead employs a carefully prepared nutrient mixture or formula to feed plants. This will act quickly and immediately on application, being absorbed without delay in solution with water through the root hairs. For practical purposes, in home or commercial hydroponics we always use fertiliser-type chemicals as the sources of nutrients. These are cheaper and easier to buy and are readily available in convenient form.

Root supports have already been mentioned. There is quite a wide choice of materials available for soilless gardeners. Unlike earth, which contains various substances, aggregates or growing media are virtually inert. They cannot be damaged by the elements and are not subject to rapid erosion as soil is. The main function of the supports is to provide an anchor for plants' roots. In addition, they also serve as a reservoir for the nutrient solution of water and fertiliser salts which contain the vital foodstuffs for growth.

DIFFERENCES FROM SOIL

The main differences between hydroponics and soil growing should now be clear to the reader. Not only is the soilless garden exact and controlled in its functioning, but it also cuts out many time-consuming and laborious jobs necessary in conventional plant cultivation. Messy manures, often smelly and slow-acting, are replaced by clean, swiftly available, mineral nutrients and the frequently unreliable earth or expensive and troublesome composts are eliminated completely in favour of an easily handled aggregate, or other supporting device. These advantages, together with many others already discussed, are what have made so many lovers of plants turn to hydroponics as the ideal system for use in the home.

CHAPTER III

Simple Growing Units

Soilless garden units for simple household hydroponics are easy to set up. The method recommended here for beginners is scientifically designed to give good results. At the same time, every effort has been made to avoid any complicated equipment which home gardeners or housewives might find a little difficult to use. Individual preferences and local needs often vary very much and therefore the final choice of containers or receptacles for plants may well be left to personal taste and convenience. A hydroponic unit is made up of the following parts: (a) *container*, also called a bed or trough, though frequently pots and miscellaneous receptacles are employed; (b) the *aggregate* or growing medium, which is placed in the container and provides support for the roots; and (c) *water supply*. In most installations the plant food, in the form of fertiliser salts, is added to the water to constitute the nutrient solution. This is then applied to the beds, troughs or pots in normal watering. To work the soilless garden you will also need a few items of standard pattern, such as a can, a small hand fork, a kitchen balance, and some string or twine to tie up taller plants. In this chapter we will discuss the different parts of the home hydroponic unit, how to set them up, and suggest some positions for plant growing in and around the house.

(a) CONTAINERS

Various kinds of containers may be used for home growing without soil. Shallow boxes, pots, bowls, old kitchen sinks, and other receptacles are quite satisfactory. It is not difficult to construct troughs of any desired size from bricks and mortar or concrete. Usually, a depth of six inches is best. This allows adequate room for root development and is not too tall. Hydroponic plants, in fact, require less space or depth for rooting than do soil-grown ones, because their roots are more compact and have ample supplies of essential nutrients immediately available. Containers should not be made from any material likely to prove toxic to plants. If of galvanised iron sheeting, then they should be painted with a good quality varnish or paint before use. Wooden containers may be lined with

FIG. 3 Different small-sized household containers for some hydroponics including pots, bowls, various vessels, a half-barrel and a window box.

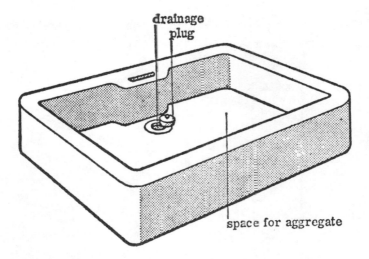

FIG. 4 How to use an old kitchen sink as a hydroponic container.

polythene, which is waterproof and can be fixed in position with drawing-pins. Ready-made plastic troughs of various types are available in shops. Other suggestions include cut-down barrels and cans, oil drums sawn in sections and even automobile tyres split into halves. Asbestos, too, makes excellent hydroponic beds. The length and width of soilless gardens will depend on the needs of the house-holder, but generally speaking it is desirable to keep the width of units to three feet or under, because otherwise it becomes difficult to attend properly to the plants growing in them. Any convenient length may be employed, to suit particular situations.

It is important to be sure that containers for hydroponics have holes in the base. In fact, only one hole of a diameter not exceeding a quarter to a half of an inch is needed in pots; in troughs, however, several holes may be desirable. If there are too many apertures, close them up with Plasticine, screwed-up wads of newspaper or wooden plugs, leaving only enough for drainage and aeration. Most plant pots, as well as some troughs offered for sale, do have holes already punched in the bottom, or else a few marks in the bases showing where you can push a pencil or skewer through to form a suitable aperture. In hydroponic gardening, the holes are only opened at certain times and are fitted with small plugs or stoppers. To catch any seepage, shallow dishes, saucers or old tin lids can be placed underneath pots, and gutters fixed beside troughs, beds or longer containers.

To make a very simple room or kitchen trough, ask your green-grocer to give you a light wooden box of the kind used for packing

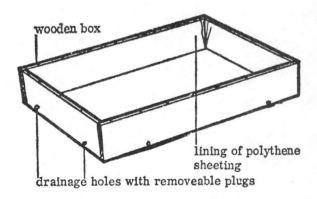

FIG. 5   A box type of container ready for filling with aggregate.

grapes, pears or large peaches. This will be about two feet long by one to one-and-a-half feet wide and some six inches deep. Box sizes do vary, but these measurements are fairly average ones. Place the box on a table or similar stand. Then take some polythene plastic sheeting, or opened bags of this material, like those used for wrapping different heavy goods. Line the box carefully with the waterproof plastic, turning it up at the sides and ends and fixing it in position with drawing pins to the top edges of the box. Now, using a gimlet or sharp skewer, make small holes half-an-inch from the bottom of the box, two in each side and two at one end only. Put two small stones or a strip of thin wood under the other end, so as to raise it not more than three-quarters of an inch. Finally, put little plugs in each of the holes you made. Your hydroponic trough or container will now be ready and can be filled with aggregate. It is quite easy to make lots of such simple units, arranging them in series or as may be convenient.

(b) AGGREGATES

Once you have chosen your containers or made them from available materials, the next job is to fill them with aggregate or growing medium. Quite a number of different aggregates are satisfactory for hydroponics. Very often, however, it may be most economical to use a growing medium which is in plentiful supply locally and will cost little or nothing. For example, sand, gravel, or small pebbles can frequently be gathered near the home, without expense, while cinders from coal fires only require washing to make them suitable for soilless gardening. Here is a list of common aggregates employed by hydroponicists.

Sand

The best sands for hydroponic gardening are fairly coarse ones, especially river or beach sands. Too fine sands are liable to become waterlogged, thus preventing good aeration of the plants' roots. In technical terms, we classify sand size on the basis of mesh, that is to say sieve measurement. A sieve size range of from 14 to 100 mesh is highly satisfactory, consisting of several grades. Sands with a uniform particle diameter of under 30 mesh should not be used alone, but should be mixed with a proportion of coarser materials. At Jealott's Hill Research Station in Berkshire, maintained by

Imperial Chemical Industries Ltd., the late Dr W. G. Templeman used the following mixture of sands for hydroponic growth of plants:

Garside's Grade 2L

Sieve size	%
Mesh 10	1·51
Mesh 10–20	20·45
Mesh 20–30	24·24
Mesh 30–40	34·09
Mesh 40–50	9·85
Mesh 50–80	8·35
Mesh 80–100	1·51
	100·00

At Habbaniyah, the former Royal Air Force station in Iraq, the sand used for hydroponics was obtained from the lakeshore and contained approximately twenty-five per cent of material which graded out between 10 and 60 mesh. This allowed for excellent aeration. In Aruba, in the Netherlands West Indies, coarser sands have been employed with much success, even those having a particle size of one-sixteenth to one-eighth of an inch. For home growing purposes, under most conditions, sands should not contain more than half of their volume of material below 30 mesh sieve size, with the balance made up of larger grains. In colder and wetter places coarser sands give better aeration, but in hot localities or positions they will dry out more rapidly. Advice on sand sizes and qualities may usually be obtained from builders' merchants and garden centres, which sell this material.

Gravels

These are small rounded or broken stones and for practical purposes include pebbles, crushed rocks of various types, crushed limestone and corals, silica gravel, river gravel, beach shingle, slate chippings and haydite or burnt shale. The particle size of gravels ranges generally from one-sixteenth to half-an-inch in diameter. The best types have sizes of from one-eighth to three-eighths of an inch. For home hydroponics, using the simple method of growth, better results may be obtained by employing gravel aggregates that contain a reasonable proportion of finer material. The Royal Horticultural Society of England conducted some trials in soilless cultivation in 1942–43 and found that a growing medium prepared as follows gave excellent development of plants:

Gravel Mixture for Soilless Culture, screened with
Institute of Mining and Metallurgy standard sieves

Aggregate	size in mm	%
Coarse gravel	over 2	25
Fine gravel	0.4–2	30
Coarse sand	0.18–0.4	40
Fine sand	under 0.007	5
		100

Similar mixtures were also made up consisting of thirteen per cent of coarse gravels and sixty-two per cent of finer materials. In India and parts of Africa, it is normal to prepare growing media for hydroponics by mixing together about five parts of gravel with a grade of from one quarter to five-eighths of an inch and three parts of sand by volume.

Broken Bricks

Bricks may be broken up into small pieces quite easily, using heavy hammers. It is best to reduce them to a maximum grade of half-an-inch sized particles, which will give also a substantial proportion of smaller chips and brick dust. Put all these, well mixed together, into the beds or containers to serve as the growing medium.

Vermiculite

This product is obtained from naturally occurring desposits located in various parts of the world. It is classified as a hydrated magnesium aluminium silicate. The name comes from the Latin, *vermis*, a worm. The ore is made up of two materials, vermiculite and biotite. In the former, the scales are bonded together with water and in the latter with potassium. On heating to a temperature of about 2000° F the water is converted into steam, which expands the material to from twelve to fifteen times its original volume. The resulting product is sterile, light in weight, highly absorbent and retains water and air. These properties make vermiculite very useful for hydroponic gardening. If you look closely at the small particles you will see that they curl slightly and do look rather like short worms. Various grades of vermiculite are available in stores, garden centres and from horticultural suppliers. It is best to ask for the standard garden grade, which is often sold under proprietary names such as Exflor, Vermicult, or Collite. Vermiculite has given good results in household soilless gardens, but it is generally best to mix it with an equal amount of sand because its high water retaining properties may sometimes keep plants too damp during winter periods.

Cinders

Many types of cinders can be used for growing plants without soil. Soft and hard coal cinders should be soaked in water for twenty-four hours and then washed clean before placing in the hydroponic containers. This process is called 'leaching'. In old gardens one can often find leach-troughs or tubs. The finer ash should not be discarded, but after drying, should be mixed in with the bigger cinders to constitute a composite growing medium. Other kinds of cinders include volcanic ash, which is in plentiful supply in countries like Grand Canary or near active or dormant volcanic zones. Charcoal is another type of cinder and makes a good hydroponic aggregate, though often rather costly and hard to get in industrialised areas. Lava can also be mentioned under this heading, it can be broken up into a useful growth medium. Pumice is, of course, a glassy lava, so full of gas cavities as to float in water sometimes.

Peat

This should not be utilised by itself as a hydroponic growing medium since its unbalanced composition may give rise to patches of poor plant development. However, small amounts of peat can usefully be added to sand and vermiculite aggregates, to loosen them up, as well as to improve aeration. The addition of between twenty-five and forty per cent by volume of peat moss to coarse sand helps moisture retention.

Miscellaneous growing media

As well as the various materials already mentioned a few others have been used with success by soilless gardeners in different areas. British Columbian growers often employ sawdust, either alone or in mixtures. Plastic chips, expanded perlite—an acid volcanic glass, pebble phosphate rock from Florida, and leca, a lightweight expanded clay aggregate have all given good results. Leca is a product of cement manufacture and is formed of numbers of hard, round pebbles with some dust-like residues. It absorbs up to four times its own volume of water. At the present time, this aggregate is produced by seventeen manufacturing plants in Europe and South America and is in quite plentiful supply. Readers may well find that in their districts sources of alternative aggregates, not mentioned here, exist, quite suitable for hydroponics. It is always worthwhile trying such growing media, especially when they are easily available and cost little.

SOURCES OF AGGREGATES

Very often you may have access to natural sources of growing media for hydroponics. For example, sand is freely available near the sea and often inland. Small stones can also be collected, while cinders are residues left from fires. Other sources include quarries, rock falls, and volcanic outpourings. In other cases, aggregates of different kinds may be obtained from builders' merchants, garden stores and similar suppliers.

Leca aggregate is supplied by: Leca (Great Britain) Ltd., 16 Old Queen Street, London S.W.1 and branches in England.

Sources of vermiculite in the United Kingdom include:
Dupre Vermiculite Ltd., Tamworth Road, Hertford, Hertfordshire.
Vermipeat Ltd., 1 Bath Road, Bitton, near Bristol.

In other areas of the world, local firms can offer supplies. If in any difficulty it may be useful to contact the nearest horticultural or agricultural advisory office.

WATER SUPPLY

Most waters are quite suitable for home soilless gardening. Our supplies come from a wide number of sources, including rivers, reservoirs, wells, boreholes, and sometimes distilled sea water. The first test is that if the water is good for drinking by human beings or animals then it will be satisfactory for plants. At one time, it was thought that if the salt content of a water exceeded two thousand five hundred parts per million then it would be too saline for garden flowers and vegetables. Recent research work in North Africa and Israel has shown this to be incorrect. So long as there is good drainage and free movement of salty water through the growing medium plants will tolerate very saline water, even sea water, for indefinite periods. The late Dr Hugo Boyko, President of the World Academy of Art and Science, was responsible for most of these investigations, which have very important implications for the extension of hydroponics in desert regions where the only large water resources that exist are often salty or may have to be drawn from the sea through pipelines. In the light of this work, we can qualify the remark about suitability of water for plant growing by adding that many supplies that would be unpalatable for drinking can do very well for raising flowers and vegetables.

Water containing a lot of magnesium and calcium salts is termed 'hard'. Both this kind of water and 'soft' waters are quite suitable for hydroponics. Sometimes, waters do contain small amounts of salts that might injure plants. For example, excess chlorine will cause a hardening of growth. To deal with this, it is best to filter the water through a tank packed with straw, dried leaves, or grass and then allow it to stand in the open for a few hours. Rain water is in theory pure, but in actual practice it contains minute amounts of dissolved nitrogen, oxygen, and carbon dioxide, as well as certain impurities, especially near large industrial cities. These are not generally of any great significance in hydroponics. Municipal supplies, that is to say, ordinary tap water, have been filtered and treated. The chlorine content varies, but is unlikely to be excessive for soilless culture.

For small household units, simple trials of water can be made by placing a few cut stems or flowers in a glassful over a period of a day or two. If no ill effects are observed, the water may be presumed satisfactory for use. These days it is quite simple to obtain analyses of most water supplies from the local municipality or city, or in country areas from the agricultural departments. It is always interesting for the soilless gardener to know what type of water he or she is working with.

The application of water to hydroponic containers, or irrigation, as it is also called, can be carried out in simple soilless gardens by using cans, ordinary jugs, or hosepipes. In larger installations it is done by means of systems of pipes and sprays, chiefly of course in order to save labour costs.

SETTING UP A HYDROPONIC UNIT

Having selected the particular kind of container that you prefer
—and this can be a plant pot, trough, box or other receptacle, as we
have already seen—the first thing to do is to fill it with the chosen
aggregate. For beginners, there is little doubt that the most easily
managed growing medium is a mixture of coarse sand with some
larger material, such as broken bricks, gravel, cinders, vermiculite
or perhaps leca. Alternatively, you can use freshly broken bricks
or rocks, blending both the chips and the dust well together to form
a composite aggregate. If you decide on sand and a separate second
material, here is the procedure. Take two parts sand and three parts
of the larger aggregate, the grade of which should not exceed one

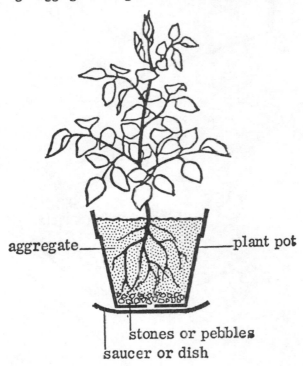

FIG. 6 Setting up a hydroponic pot. The drainage hole is covered
by a layer of an inch or so of pebbles, broken flowerpots or small
stones to prevent the growing medium being washed out into the
saucer.

quarter-of-an-inch, measuring the amounts by volume, and mix them thoroughly. Do not weigh the quantities because the density is different, but use a tin or bucket to get the correct amounts. Before you place this hydroponic aggregate in the container spread about an inch or so of clean, broken flower pot pieces, small stones or

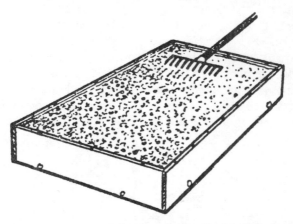

FIG. 7 After filling to within about half-an-inch of the top, rake the growing medium smooth.

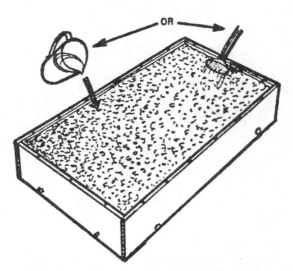

FIG. 8 Moisten the aggregate with water using either a jug or a sprinkler.

pebbles on the bottom of the receptacle. This will prevent any of the growing medium washing down into the drainage holes and perhaps blocking them up. It will also ensure better circulation of air. The rest of the container should then be filled with the prepared aggregate to within half-an-inch of the top. Firm it down gently and smooth it over making sure that the surface is quite level.

As soon as the hydroponic container has been filled with the chosen aggregate mixture, water it carefully with enough clean water to moisten the growing medium. This will settle it in place. If you

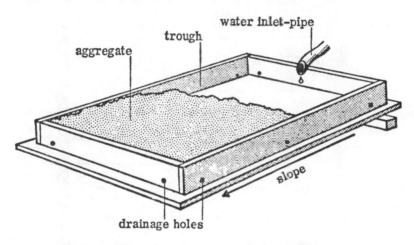

FIG. 9 The different parts of the hydroponic unit. Here we see how the various features are combined to set up a soilless garden. *Note:* A gutter can be placed around the bottoms of the sides to catch any seepage or a tray put under the trough will do the same job satisfactorily.

have not done so already put the unit in the position where you intend to operate it. The watering may be done with a can, jug, or pipe, but it is much easier if you fit a rose or sprinkler to whatever appliance you use to spread the liquid evenly over the whole surface of the growing medium. About half-an-hour after this watering, pull out the plugs from the drainage holes and allow any excess moisture to run off into saucers placed underneath receptacles like pots, or into trays and gutters for troughs, boxes and beds. The plugs should be replaced when the seepage stops.

The hydroponic unit will now be ready for sowing or planting.

In the following chapters we shall discuss these tasks, as well as how to apply the vital nutrients and the general care of crops. But before dealing with these important operations, let us examine the question of suitable sites in or around the home and in the amateur's garden for soilless culture installations. One of the main advantages of hydroponics is that it can be started in places where ordinary soil growing would be impracticable. This opens the way to a very wide

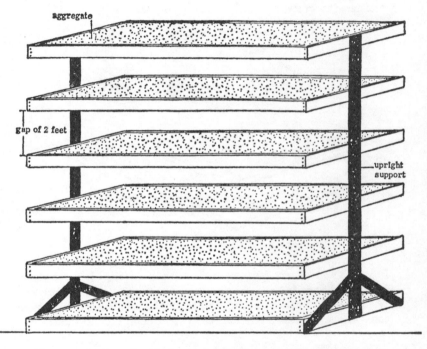

FIG. 10 A tier of troughs or boxes for growing quick-maturing salads in the kitchen by means of hydroponics. By nailing strips of wood to the ends of sets of boxes to provide uprights for support, simple effective stands can be erected rapidly and cheaply.

selection of positions for soilless units. Flowers and house plants will grow very well inside rooms, on window ledges, along balconies, or in hanging containers. Backyards, flat rooftops, the sides of paths and passageways are other obvious sites. For the kitchen, tiers of troughs for vegetables and quick maturing salads are quite practicable. Outside beds can be established on any open space, in existing gardens, or on waste ground. In cold regions these may be covered with polythene sheeting on frames or cloches for protection, while in the tropics matting shades will provide an effective safeguard against the rays of the hot sun. Roofing-felt is also satisfactory for the prevention of excessive surface temperatures causing scorch in hydroponic beds or troughs and it can, incidentally, be employed as well to make good containers if attached to wooden or brick supports. The number of possible sites for soilless gardening is almost unlimited. A little ingenuity and thought on the part of the householder or amateur gardener will result in space-saving arrangements and adaptations of lasting value. Here are a few examples that have come to the author's notice during recent years—

One New Zealand gardener, living near Napier, commenting on the possibilities of the pumice areas in that country, said: 'Pumice is a warm porous material, rich in potash. Underneath the pumice land is thermal steam, making a natural hot-house. Hydroponics on this land, combined with our sunlight, are all we need to grow anything anywhere at any time.' Another grower, resident in Guildford, Surrey, England, described his early beginnings as follows: 'I commenced hydroponics in a disused aquarium, two feet by one foot by one foot deep, having drilled five holes a quarter of an inch in diameter for drainage in the base. It proved very satisfactory for plants and I had excellent results with tomatoes and a melon.' Later on, this amateur built troughs on the staging inside his greenhouse. The Ahmedabad Municipal Corporation, in India, completed in 1955 a new museum building, designed by the well-known architect, Le Corbusier, with a large top terrace specially constructed for hydroponics. This terrace was intended for the instruction and entertainment of visitors. It is waterproofed and the soilless beds are made of concrete. A London stockbroker, living in Chelsea, grows regular supplies of vegetables on his kitchen roof, using receptacles made from wooden boards with linings of roofing-felt. His wife also maintains a large number of decorative hydroponic house plants and indoor flowers. Near Dar-Es-Salaam in Tanzania, a garden produce company sited their units in a coconut plantation, which provided partial shade for salad crops such as lettuce and cucumbers. The beds were constructed from old cement bags laids on sand and painted with several coats of asphalt. An enterprising Rhodesian farmer of Bulawayo has adopted a very ingenious way of siting his hydroponic garden. He says: 'I built my house in difficult soil and to get good foundations I went down over eight feet. I converted this into a basement with a suspended floor, so that I now have an area of over fifteen hundred square feet with a clearance of seven feet and no pillars to worry me. This basement is wired for both power and light. Ventilation is provided by slots in the walls above ground level. The outside walls of the house are cavity ones, and weep holes allow the basement air to go up through the cavities to the roof. I have a big home-made ventilator in this and as the roof is made of iron sheets it acts as a gigantic pump. The result of all this is that the basement is always sweet and fresh and has an annual temperature range of from 64° to 70° F. I am putting a fifteen foot apron around the house and converting both it and the basement area into a hydroponic unit. The basement will be frost-free and enable me to grow out-of-season crops. I can use artificial lighting. My chief interests are early potatoes, lettuce, tomatoes, watercress, various bulb flowers like hyacinths, chrysanthemums, and possibly roses.

So long as hydroponic units are kept in positions where the plants receive enough air, together with adequate light—natural or artificial —and a supply of water is available, the actual site itself is of secondary importance. When you start soilless gardening you will probably know just where you would like to put your containers. A little ingenuity will do the rest. Remember, however, that all sites must be clean and free from disease-carrying rubbish. Dusty and windy places do not favour good growth and plants will need protection by means of screens in such positions otherwise they may suffer serious damage. In houses, take care that gas leaks do not occur in the vicinity of hydroponic containers.

SUPPLEMENTARY NEEDS

In addition to the main items for preparing the simple growing unit, a few other things will be required for hydroponic home gardens. Most of these may be already available in the house. For instance a kitchen weighing scale or balance for measuring out nutrients; an old teaspoon; a hand fork for smoothing over the surface of the aggregate or moving seedlings and transplanting, as desired; a jug or preferably a small watering can fitted with a thin spout and rose or a hosepipe with a sprinkler attached for watering and applying the plant feeding solution. Further helpful accessories can include scissors or sharp knife for pruning and cutting, dark green twine and string for tying plants, bamboo canes for staking, a soft brush for dusting hairy-leaved ornamentals or pollinating cucumbers and tomatoes, and any similar useful equipment that may come in handy from time to time.

Containers

A wide range of containers are offered by Stewart Plastics Ltd., Purley Way, Croydon, Surrey, England.

Self-watering pots, of value in household work for hydroponics are supplied through garden shops by some firms. Notable amongst these are the Marmax self-watering camel pots and the various series made by the Horticultural Division of Simplex of Cambridge Ltd., Sawston, Cambridge, England.

CHAPTER IV

Feeding your Plants

Healthy plants demand ample supplies of nourishing foodstuffs and where these are deficient or unbalanced flowers and vegetables will grow slowly or not at all. The symptoms of food shortage are well known to scientists and experienced gardeners. It is the job of hydroponics to ensure that crops receive optimum quantities of plant nutrients, in the right proportions, throughout their useful lives. In the preceding chapters we have learnt the basic facts about soilless gardening, what the system sets out to achieve and how green plants grow. In addition, we have also discussed the various kinds of containers suitable for home hydroponics and the aggregates or growing media that can be used to fill them and provide support for roots. Now the time has come to talk about the mineral salts or fertilisers that supply the essential plant nutrients. It has already been explained that when a correctly balanced chemical mixture or formula is dissolved in the proper amount of water it forms a nutrient solution capable of sustaining crop growth. Several hundred different formulae have been developed by different scientists and institutions concerned with soilless cultivation over the years, but they all have the same object: to supply plants with the vital food elements, such as nitrogen, potash, phosphorus, calcium, sulphur, magnesium, iron and other minor or trace nutrients. Today, it is generally accepted that the actual choice of mineral salts for fertiliser mixtures is of little significance, provided a balanced concentration of the necessary elements is assured. Of course, care must be taken not to include incompatible chemicals in a formula or to choose those that might give rise to undesirable effects. Given these guidelines, what then becomes of importance in practical soilless home gardening is the local availability of the nutrients and their cost. Fertiliser salts are normally cheaper than laboratory grade nutrients, therefore it pays to employ ordinary agricultural or horticultural brands. Morover, as will be explained below, since these commercial grades contain many of the minor elements such as manganese, boron, zinc, and copper as incidental impurities, it is scarcely necessary to add extra amounts of these particular nutrients to a simple hydroponic formula or mixture for household work, a fact that makes for easier maintenance and operation of units.

The amateur hydroponicist, starting soilless gardening, need only be concerned with one, or at the most, two, formulae for feeding his or her plants. Any reputable chemist or pharmacy, garden centre or horticultural supplier can easily prepare the prescriptions given in this chapter and supply them to growers in ready-made form. In fact, many firms do offer complete mixtures for use in hydroponics to the public. The question of whether to buy your nutrient mixtures ready-made or to blend your own at home is a matter of personal choice. It is quite simple to weigh out fertiliser salts in the kitchen on an ordinary balance or scales and then mix them together. It is also cheaper in the long run and adds greater interest to your hydroponic gardening. But if you are too busy to spare even the few minutes required for the task, then it may be best to copy out one or other of the simple prescriptions listed below and hand it to the nearest large chemist or garden supplier to be made up, just as if it were a medical prescription, or else buy a proprietary brand of hydroponic nutrient mixture. The fertiliser salts mentioned in the formulae recommended here should be readily available in all parts of the world, especially from agricultural and horticultural firms, shops like Woolworth's and Boots, garden stores, and other general emporia. If in any doubt, you can look up the names of fertiliser firms in your local gardening magazines and journals, or obtain advice from agricultural or horticultural departments.

NUTRIENT FORMULAE

For general use in home soilless gardens the following mixture will give excellent results.

B.M.3

Fertiliser Salt	Quantity in Ounces	Grammes	Nutrient Elements Supplied
Ammonium sulphate	10	284	Nitrogen, Sulphur
Potassium sulphate	3½	100	Potassium, Sulphur
Superphosphate	5	142	Phosphorus, Calcium
Magnesium sulphate	3	86	Magnesium, Sulphur
Iron sulphate	Enough to cover the head of a match		Iron

Another formula, differing only slightly from the one above, which has proved its worth is:

B.M.1

Fertiliser Salt	Quantity in Ounces	Grammes	Nutrient Elements Supplied
Sodium nitrate	12½	355	Nitrogen
Potassium sulphate	4	113	Potassium, Sulphur
Superphosphate	5	142	Phosphorus, Calcium
Magnesium sulphate	3½	100	Magnesium, Sulphur
Iron sulphate	Enough to cover the head of a match		Iron

A third mixture may also be mentioned, which is recommended by the United States Department of Agriculture:

A.R.S.32

Fertiliser Salt	Quantity in Ounces	Grammes	Nutrient Elements Supplied
Ammonium sulphate	1½	43	Nitrogen, Sulphur
Potassium nitrate	9	255	Nitrogen, Potassium
Monocalcium phosphate	4	113	Phosphorus, Calcium
Magnesium sulphate	6	170	Magnesium, Sulphur
Calcium sulphate	7	198	Calcium, Sulphur
Iron sulphate	Enough to cover the nail of your little finger		Iron

Note: In the above three mixtures, trace nutrients, including manganese, boron, zinc, and copper will be present as impurities in the fertilisers listed and probably in the water supply.

You will notice that the quantities of the individual fertiliser salts vary in each mixture. This is largely because different salts contain different percentage proportions of the range of nutrient elements. The fertilisers are, in fact, merely the vehicles through which the elements are made available to the plants' roots. Hydroponic formulae are compiled according to standard calculations, which will be found in more advanced books, or works on agricultural chemistry.

PREPARING MIXTURES

The prescriptions listed above should be prepared in the following manner.

Carefully weigh out on a kitchen balance the lots of the individual salts that you will see in the formula you have selected. As you do this, put them in turn in a bowl or other container, and when you have finished weighing, mix them all well together using a wooden spoon, pestle, or other blunt instrument to break down any lumps. The resulting mixture should resemble a fairly fine powder. Sometimes it is best to crush the iron sulphate separately and add it last to the mixture to ensure better distribution of this small amount of salt. The formulae must always be stored in a *dry* container, with the lid closed. Never let nutrients get damp or wet before application. This also refers to the individual fertilisers, which should be kept in a suitable store place. To prepare larger quantities of nutrient formula, simply multiply up all the ingredients to the desired amounts, using a constant number, so that the relative proportions remain the same. It is important to remember this, otherwise any alteration of the inbuilt ratios will make the mixture unbalanced.

In making up nutrient solutions for feeding plants only quite small amounts of formula are used in given quantities of water, normally about one-third of an ounce or ten grammes to one gallon of water. In practical household work, this may be regarded as a standard unheaped teaspoonful of nutrient mixture to each gallon. So you can see that the weights given in the prescriptions will go quite a long way. Instructions for nutrient solution application will be detailed more fully in the next chapter.

PROPRIETARY MIXTURES

If you decide not to prepare your own formula, but to purchase one or other of the ready-made hydroponic mixtures now available, the manufacturer's advice about quantities to apply should be followed. The following are a few of the different fertiliser compounds currently available for soilless gardening:

Phostrogen

This mixture of plant growth food for hydroponics has been recommended by the Institute of Hydroponics and is prepared by

Phostrogen Ltd., Tower House, Barmouth, North Wales. It is a fine nutrient powder specially made for home use, consisting of appropriate quantities of superphosphate, potassium nitrate, ammonium sulphate, magnesium sulphate, calcium sulphate, iron sulphate, manganese sulphate and other minor elements. Considered as a compound fertiliser formula, Phostrogen hydroponic mixture has the following analysis: nitrogen 9·7%, phosphoric acid (soluble in water) 10%, phosphoric acid (insoluble in water) 0·8%, and potassium 26·5%. Because of the purity of the mineral salts employed in the compounding of this mixture, only quite small quantities are needed for preparing the nutrient solution or plant food. The makers advise that, at full strength, one teaspoonful should be mixed in every two gallons of water to nourish seedlings and mature plants, while for seeds prior to and just after germination, a quarter-strength application is adequate, that is to say one teaspoonful of the powder to eight gallons of water, or pro rata.

Sustanum

A carrier material prepared from siliceous substances contains the plant food. When incorporated in water to form a solution, the nutrients are released for the benefit of the crops. Sustanum provides a balanced nutrient formula for the growth of flowers and vegetables. It is simple and easy to use and is made in two mixtures, one for colder climates and one for tropical areas. One of the advantages of this fertiliser mixture for hydroponics is that far fewer applications need to be given, since the material containing the plant food remains available for lengthy periods in the root zone. Sustanum for soilless home gardening may be obtained, with full instructions for application, from the manufacturers: Trace Element Fertilizers Ltd., 118 Ewell Road, Surbiton, Surrey, England.

Other Compounds

Prepared mixtures of fertiliser salts for hydroponics can be supplied by several different firms, in addition to those already mentioned. Some manufacturers include:

Hydroponic Chemical Co., Inc., Box 97-C, Copley, Ohio, U.S.A.
India Alkalies Ltd., 5 Garston Place, Calcutta, West Bengal, India. (Product—Manurin).
Chas. C. Gilbert & Co., Ivy Street, San Diego 1, California, U.S.A.

Easi-Gro Products Ltd., Dart Mills, Buckfastleigh, Devon, England.

J. A. Gordon & Son Ltd., Stonehouse, Gloucestershire, England.

Hydroponics Inc., 2039 S. Madison Avenue, Indianapolis, Indiana 46225, U.S.A.

Bowden Hydroponics, Maynard O'Connor (Pty) Ltd., Bowden, Adelaide, South Australia.

Pan Britannica Industries Ltd., Britannica House, Waltham Cross, Hertfordshire, England. (Product—Bio).

Suttons of Reading Ltd., Reading, Berkshire, England.

No doubt more products will come on to the market as time passes and local enquiries will usually reveal further sources of supply.

RATE OF APPLICATION

This will be discussed fully in the next chapter. When using the simple home method of soilless gardening, the aggregate in the containers must always be kept moist with nutrient solution to ensure good plant growth. Solution strengths—that is the quantity of fertiliser mixture to be added to the water—have been mentioned already. The number of applications of solution to hydroponic receptacles will alter slighty according to local climatic conditions, obviously being more frequent in a hot, dry place than in a cool, damp one. Normally, from two or three times weekly to daily, depending on situation and factors like temperature and evaporation, will suffice. If the formulae are prepared carefully and the correct quantities added to the water, the nutrient solution cannot harm plants, as long as the roots are not deprived of aeration, no matter how often, within reason, it is applied.

CHAPTER V

Sowing and General Care

Once the hydroponic containers have been filled with aggregate and given their first watering with plain water, sowing or planting may commence. The growing medium should have been well dampened, being just as moist as a wet sponge that has been lightly wrung out. The drainage holes will be closed with the plugs that you have provided, after the initial aeration of the aggregate, as explained in Chapter III. All will now be ready for the next step.

SOWING

Good sowing helps plants considerably in their early lives and indeed throughout flowering and fruiting. In hydroponics, the task of seeding is made much easier than in soil gardening because the aggregate is of generally even texture throughout and at the right degree of moisture, as well as being free from contamination. Moreover, only a light covering of growing medium is necessary to conceal the germinating seeds from the light.

Avoid watering newly-sown seeds excessively; the aggregate around them should be as moist as a lightly wrung-out sponge. This permits enough moisture to reach the germinating seeds, while allowing essential aeration. Normally, large seeds are put into small holes made with the end of a pencil, or something like the handle of a spoon, in the aggregate, about half-an-inch deep, at intervals, so that when the growing medium is smoothed back over them they will have a covering of approximately half that amount. It is not necessary to bury seeds deeply in hydroponic gardening. When sowing smaller ones, the easiest way is to remove a little aggregate from the surface, sprinkle the seeds carefully and then replace the growing medium on top of them, to give a thin but effective covering. Mixing very fine seeds with some dry sand or 'filler' assists in securing even distribution. Pelleted seeds may now be bought in many places and are extremely simple to sow. They can be inserted into the aggregate at appropriate intervals.

Usually, the maximum depth at which most flower and vegetable seeds should be planted should be such as not to have more than a quarter of an inch of aggregate over them. Seeds need to germinate in the dark under a protective, but light, cover of the thin layer of surface growing medium. In hydroponics, it is possible to plant much closer than in soil, since ample nutrients are available. However, the number of seeds placed in any single soilless garden container will depend upon individual preferences and the need to allow sufficient light to reach each plant. Therefore, follow standard distances in general, remembering that you can reduce the spaces between plants by up to fifty per cent, if the circumstances warrant this, under favourable conditions, and you want a closer or thicker stand or display.

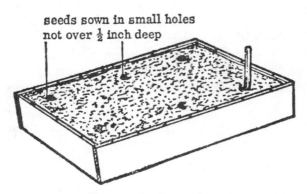

seeds sown in small holes
not over ½ inch deep

FIG. 11   Sowing seeds.

Let us take for an example the sowing of a hydroponic trough or container about two feet long by one-and-a-half feet wide, set up by the kitchen window. To begin with, you want to try easy-to-grow crops like lettuces or dwarf tomatoes. Take twelve good seeds of the plants you prefer and sow them by pushing them gently down into the moist aggregate with a small stick. Do not bury them more than half-an-inch at the most. A hydroponic trough of this size will have enough space for at least six plants. So put the seeds two together, at equal intervals, with three groups of two each down one side of the container and the same number along the other side. See that they are covered nicely by the aggregate and not left exposed to the light. When the seeds have germinated and are growing well, pull out the weaker one in each group and discard it, to permit the strong plant to develop by itself. The object of sowing two seeds together is because sometimes a seed may fail to grow well, and it saves time to have a second one ready to take its place.

When sowing has been completed, smooth over the surface of the aggregate in the containers, making sure that no seeds are exposed. If one or two are, push them down gently into the growing medium so that they are properly covered. It is a good plan to give a very light watering soon after sowing. This can be done using the technique already recommended—a watering can fitted with a rose or sprinkler, a jug with a sieve to pour the water through gently or even an old teapot. Rubber sprinklers are easily obtainable from garden shops and can be slipped over the spout. After a few days or a week or two, depending on the kind of seeds sown, germination will be noticed. Tiny green plumules or shoots will appear above the surface of the growing medium. If you have sown too many seeds in a container, remove or thin them out or transplant them to other receptacles when they are about three-quarters to one inch high. A kitchen or small hand fork is excellent for this job. Also it is easy to rearrange the tiny plants in different positions at this stage, if desired, in the

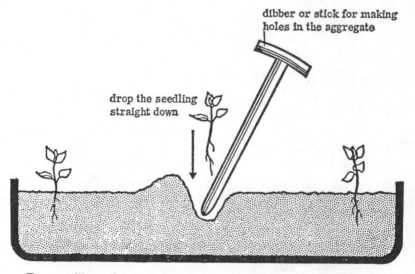

FIG. 12 Transplanting a seedling. After making a small hole in the aggregate, drop it in carefully with roots nicely extended, not bunched up, then gently push back the growing medium around it so that the young plant stands firmly.

pot or bed. Always be gentle and careful not to damage the tender seedlings; harsh pulling breaks the roots. Properly moved, there will be no check at all to hydroponic plants.

If you wish to use young seedlings, probably bought from a garden shop or nursery, instead of seeding your containers, be sure to wash off any soil adhering to their roots before planting them in a hydroponic trough. This can be done by holding them under a slowly running tap. Make small holes in the aggregate at equal intervals, as for seed sowing, drop in the seedlings, taking care that their roots are not turned up and gently rake back the growing medium around them. The stems should be firm and steady and not left to wobble about. Many hydroponic gardeners like to raise their own seedlings in separate boxes of sand and then transplant them into the main containers later.

SOLUTION APPLICATION

Assuming that you have seeded or planted your hydroponic pots or troughs and given them a very light sprinkling of water to smooth down the surface, the task now is to ensure that the growing medium is kept constantly moist with nutrient solution containing the vital plant foodstuffs. We have already seen how the fertilising formula is prepared and if you have not already chosen the one you mean to use and mixed it up, or bought a proprietary formula, you should do this immediately. Take the correct quantity of nutrient mixture, that is one-third of an ounce (ten grammes) or a level teaspoonful and dissolve it in a gallon of water. Stir it well so that no residues remain at the bottom of the can, jug, or other vessel. If you think, or know, that you will require more than a gallon of solution, mix up larger amounts by increasing the weight or number of teaspoonfuls of formula and the quantity of water. Naturally, bigger cans or vessels will be wanted for greater quantities of nutrient solution. In large hydroponic units, tanks are employed for mixing up the solution. For proprietary mixtures, follow the manufacturer's instructions exactly.

The day after sowing or planting the hydroponic containers —or even the same day if the weather or site is warm—apply the first dose of nutrient solution by watering it well over the surface of the aggregate. Sprinkle it evenly so that all parts of the trough or pot get fair amounts. You can of course use a hosepipe fitted with a spray or rose in bigger garden units to save time and labour. The aim is to maintain the growing medium in a continually damp condition, resembling a wet sponge that has been gently wrung out. The importance of good solution application or irrigation cannot be over-emphasised. Make further applications at necessary intervals so that the growing medium does not dry out at any time. At no period, either, should it become waterlogged—that is there must be no excess of surplus solution standing on the surface. Every few days

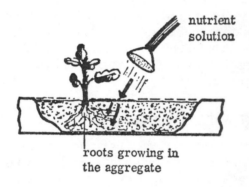

nutrient
solution

roots growing in
the aggregate

Fig. 13 Applying nutrient solution to plants. Enough is used at regular intervals, depending on the season of the year and room conditions, to keep the aggregate as moist as a damp sponge that has been lightly wrung out. Avoid overwatering or too wet a growing medium, as well as excessive dryness.

remove the plugs in the drainage holes or the Plasticine seals for a short while to allow any unused water or solution inside the bottom of the containers to seep out into the saucers or trays and gutters provided to catch it. This also makes it possible for extra air to move through the aggregate from the open holes to the surface of the medium, for the benefit of the roots. Normally, an hour or two's aeration will suffice at a time. Sometimes you may find, when the weather is warm or the plants are growing in a centrally heated room, that daily applications of nutrient solution are desirable, but in general two, three or four times weekly may be enough. Do not delay the application of the plant food, it should commence not later than the day after sowing or planting and continue regularly, as often as needed, right through the lifetime of the crops.

The simplified method of home hydroponics described in this

book has been designed to ensure that plants are neither overfed nor underfed, as they often may be in ordinary soil gardening. Instead, a regulated and balanced amount of nutrients is given to provide for good and rapid growth. Naturally, quite a lot depends also on the preparation of the containers the necessary drainage holes and their usage and the correct filling with aggregate. We have discussed suitable types of containers and how to make or obtain them in Chapter III. Further information on how to manage the drainage will be given below. The operations of watering and feeding plants have been combined into a single task by applying the nutrients in solution. Provided the instructions are adhered to, plants will not be damaged or starved at any time. The quantity of solution that you prepare at intervals will of course depend on the size of your soilless garden. As growth proceeds and the seedlings get taller and change into big plants the frequency of solution applications may be increased. Take care always to employ a sprinkler or rose on the watering-can, jug or hosepipe, so that the surface of the aggregate is not unduly disturbed. In summer months, especially in gardens outside or in warm houses, the application of plant food may be carried out daily or every other day, although conditions vary and it is not possible to stipulate the exact times. During the winter or cold periods, longer intervals between applications will be practicable, because evaporation will be less.

The golden rule is to see that the aggregate in the hydroponic containers is always as moist as a damp sponge that has been squeezed out lightly.

This bears repeating and must be remembered if good results are to be obtained. If it is kept like this, first-class growth and healthy development will follow. In using the nutrient solution you are providing both water and foodstuff together, a process that saves both work and time.

Remember, never overwater with nutrient solution; this prevents air moving through the root zone and may cause wilting and death of the plants. Watch for any excess moisture and open the drainage holes to let it seep out. Once every week or ten days it is advisable to flush through the aggregate gently by pouring some plain water (without added nutrient fertilisers) onto the surface through a sprinkler or sprayer. This will flow down, carrying away any accumulation of unused plant food, and it should be permitted to run off through the drainage apertures and then discarded. Don't forget to replace the coverings or plugs in the holes before making the next application of fresh solution. For house and conservatory plants, try to use water and solution at room or greenhouse temperature. Very hard waters can be treated with a little commercial water softener. Rain water is ideal, but very heavily chlorinated water is best left to stand in a bucket for a day before application. Plants will benefit from periodic spraying of the leaves with clean water to wash off any dust. During the resting seasons of foliage types reduce watering or irrigation with solution considerably. Another point to note is that if you let solution or water stand or lie too long on leaves when they are exposed to strong sunshine severe scorching may occur. In the tropics, overhead shades in hydroponic units will stop this sort of damage to crops. Morning watering is preferable in unheated rooms in winter months.

LIGHT

Light is vital to plant growth, but different species vary in their demands for illumination, as every gardener knows. It is advisable to keep your hydroponic units in the best light you can, preferably near windows in the case of indoor installations, especially in winter time. White or cream-coloured walls and ceilings give better light reflection in poorly-lit rooms. Leaves and stems will bend towards the source of light, a phenomenon called phototropism causing plants to grow in a lopsided manner in certain situations, so pots and other containers may have to be turned around at intervals. Young seedlings should not be exposed to bright sun for very long periods. Where sites are too dark, it is quite simple to install forty watt 'daylight' type fluorescent tube lighting, with reflectors, to supplement the ordinary electric bulbs. These tubes do not emit as much heat as filament lamps and so will not cause leaf burning. They are also pleasanter for general home use. Plants can be kept within a distance of a foot or two of fluorescent lighting, but should not be near ordinary bulbs.

AIR

Together with air, we also have to consider humidity. Ventilation in closed hydroponic units or household installations is important. There must be ample circulation of fresh air, but draughts, gases, dust and smoke are harmful to plants. However, modern gas appliances, properly fitted, are stated to be quite safe and should not emit any noxious fumes. Fires and radiators dry the atmosphere, so that it becomes necessary to raise the humidity in order to keep conditions healthy. This can be done by having a pail or pan of water standing in an inconspicuous place in a room, by spraying leaves with a syringe or sometimes wiping them carefully with a damp sponge or moist cloth or by using an electric humidifier. Steam from kitchens and bathrooms also helps, quite often, to improve the humidity in houses. It is worth remembering that too low an air moisture causes the death of many household plants and greenhouse flowers and fruits. The amount of desirable moisture in the atmosphere is assessed by categories of relative humidity. These are: *high*, over 70%; *moderate*, 50% to 70%; and *low*, under 50%. Excess humidity encourages the spread of disease.

TEMPERATURE

Generally, most plants prefer an even degree of warmth, without great fluctuations. Provided the range is between 50° and 75° F, the vast majority will do well. In rooms and houses in cool places the amounts of light and moisture in the air are not excessive and the same thing applies in hot, dry or arid districts. Too high temperatures with poor light and considerable dryness usually result in poor growth and shrivelled-up foliage. Up to an optimum, plant growth may be improved by increases in warmth. A fall in temperature normally reduces development, while at or below freezing point death of many plants occurs. Most species have been accustomed for countless generations to certain limits of heat and cold, and though it is possible to acclimatise plants in new areas, the process of so doing is often wearisome and slow. The temperature of plants tends to follow that of their surroundings, but it may be higher or lower, owing to the fact that vegetation responds more gradually to heat changes than does air. Daily alterations are commonplace, while wind, cloud and seasonal differences exert significant influences. For most temperate types of plants the best heat range is from 60° to 70° F, and from 75° to 90° F for tropical species. A maximum of as much as 125° or 130° F can be tolerated by torrid kinds; indeed growth is known to proceed at even higher temperatures than these. Minimum temperatures vary from species to species. Some plants will be killed by frost, but others survive all the year round.

Do not put household plants near hot radiators at nights. If you think it may freeze inside rooms, in greenhouses or under cloches, then you can cover them with newspapers or cloth, and draw curtains or screens across glass or window panes in winter time. Frost is a great killer, but sun scorch and desiccation are equally fatal in hot countries, where overhead shading is often essential or outside plant houses may have to be erected in the garden or compound. Growth is generally far slower at cold periods or in times of drought, when the air moisture is extremely low, but it is often surprising how tolerant some plants may be of adverse conditions and how they adapt to new situations. In horticultural terms, temperature ranges are graded as follows: *hot*, above 80° F; *warm*, 65° to 80° F; *moderate*, 50° to 65° F; and *cold*, under 50° F. At 32° F, frost will occur, but this is unlikely inside well-built houses. Nevertheless, when room warmth or greenhouse temperatures fall as low as 45° to 35° F, the conditions become difficult for most plants, and indeed for human beings too.

CLEANING

Dust can be a problem in household hydroponic units. It prevents plants breathing properly by blocking up the pores in the leaves. It can be kept in check by syringing periodically with clean water. A soft cloth or light brush are useful for ornamental and foliage types. Always observe strict cleanliness in hydroponic home gardens, removing dead leaves, stems, bad fruits or finished blossoms at once and wiping pots and containers regularly. Rake over the aggregate from time to time lightly with a small hand fork or rake. Hygiene will pay good dividends.

DAILY WORK

The general care of simple hydroponic gardens should present no problems for beginners. There is no hard manual labour, no digging, weeding or similar tasks. The first job is to keep the soilless garden free from dirt and rubbish. Dirty conditions cause disease and insect pests will soon make an appearance if vegetable refuse is left lying around. In uncared-for greenhouses, red spider is likely to become a nuisance. The main routine duty for hydroponicists is to check the condition of the aggregate regularly in the containers and see that it is properly moist and the plants are growing vigorously. It is worth remembering that all living organisms are subject to change, so no matter how good a technical system of cultivation may be, the condition of the plants can alter from day to day. There is no substitute for careful observation. Once you get the 'feel' of hydroponics, which you will certainly acquire after a few weeks of operating a soilless garden, you will be able to sense how the crops are doing and tell at once the responses of the plants to the existing environmental and nutritional conditions. This feeling for hydroponic plants may well be the equivalent of what are popularly known as 'green fingers' in soil gardening. It is difficult to define, but it is none-the-less very real. No doubt this is why soilless cultivation is an art as well as a science. The more sensitive the grower, the better will be the results.

Day by day observations of nutrient solution needs, which will vary according to the time of the year, the particular plants growing, and the location of the hydroponic garden are vital to good management. Such factors as air moisture, strength of wind, temperature range and ventilation may be very significant. The aggregate or growing medium should be at the right degree of moistness. Excessive wetness stops proper aeration, while if the root crowns or tops are waterlogged the crops will soon die. Improper aeration quickly becomes apparent in hydroponic troughs or pots. The plants assume a tired look—that of age prematurely imposed upon youth. It is easily detected after a little experience. Regular checking of light, warmth and other changes is most beneficial. In very hot, dry weather, shades should be spread over hydroponic gardens, particularly outside ones. When heavy rain occurs, protection is desirable through some form of canopy to stop excessive flooding of the containers. Moderate rain or showers will irrigate beds or troughs quite satisfactorily and offer no problems, so long as they do not dilute the nutrient solution present in the growing medium too much. You will soon see if this has happened after a few days, when growth slows up or the crops look a bit pale in colour. To adjust the deficiency, simply put screens over the unit and apply extra solution, excluding rain for a period until the plants look better. In greenhouses or where plants are sited in picture-windows, attention will need to be paid to the light conditions, opening or closing shades as required.

As the time of harvesting vegetables or picking flowers and fruits approaches, growers should make frequent inspections of the condition of the plants and decide when they are ripe or ready for collection. It is both interesting and helpful to keep records and notes about your hydroponic garden. Nothing is too insignificant to enter on such charts. A well-kept notebook becomes in time almost a text in itself and constitutes a valuable guide for future work. The dates of sowing or planting can be written on labels attached to each container. Inside houses or in greenhouses, plants like tomatoes and cucumbers will need to be pollinated to ensure good fruiting. This may be done by gentle spraying with clean water at warm air temperature or by rubbing the flowers very gently and carefully with a piece of soft cottonwool.

Transplanting in hydroponics is simple. The seedlings or young plants should be removed gently with a small fork from the aggregate and inserted in holes made with a pencil end, a piece of stick, or a thin dibber, in their new situations. Smooth back the growing medium around the roots, so that they stand firmly. Apply a little solution at once and there will be no check in growth. Repotting can be done by up-ending the container, holding the plant and aggregate around its roots securely with the hand, and then placing the whole mass in the new pot or other receptacle. If these containers are larger than the old ones, add a little extra aggregate to fill them properly. Repotting or replanting may have to be done if the roots of perennials grow down into the drainage holes, or if the plant is obviously too large for its trough. Pruning and training may follow standard lines. The general idea is to improve growth habits, prevent plants from straggling or getting out of hand and to prevent new branching. Aways cut out dead or diseased stems as soon as they are seen. Supports may be employed where stems are brittle or flower heads and fruit bunches or trusses are very heavy, as well as for climbers. Normal methods of staking and tying can be used. The best way of supporting hydroponic plants is to employ strings or twine attached to overhead wires. This avoids inserting canes or sticks into the growing medium.

In planting potatoes or bulbs, slightly larger holes will have to be made in the growing medium to accommodate the tubers or corms. All root crops do well in hydroponics. So does asparagus, fruits such as strawberries, vegetables like celery and chicory, and indeed any other kind of garden produce. Mushrooms are not, of course, higher plants but fungi, and special soilless composts are needed for their cultivation, details of which will be found in Chapter IX.

After plants have finished flowering or fruiting and are not of any further use, remove them from the containers, shake the aggregate off their roots and discard them. The growing medium can then be flushed well through with plain water, smoothed over and utilised immediately for new sowings or plantings. Don't waste any aggregate; it is made up of inert materials and when cleansed of any accumulated mineral salts and root debris, will continue to give good service for years. There is no rotation of crops in hydroponics and the same growing media may be employed over and over again without risk as long as these simple rules are followed. Provided enough warmth and light can be supplied from whatever sources, you can grow flowers and vegetables in the home or garden all the year round in hydroponics, irrespective of the season. This great advantage of soilless gardening—making possible the culture of plants out-of-season—is very important and constitutes a real boon for householders and amateurs. Not only can it bring considerable pleasure and enjoyment, but it also may help you to save money through growing your own produce in the home, thus avoiding the expense of buying costly out-of-season greenstuff for the family.

CARE DURING HOLIDAYS

There are several ways of treating soilless gardens, so that they can be left safely for some time while you are away. Smaller containers and pots may be placed on trays two inches deep. Pour plenty of solution into the trays so that it covers the outsides of the receptacles about an inch up, taking care first to remove the drainage hole coverings or plugs. The nutrient solution will then ascend through the holes into the aggregate by capillary attraction and become available to the plants' roots. Pieces of slightly damp crumpled-up newspaper may also be placed over the surface of the growing medium in the containers. As soon as you return, put the containers back into their normal positions, pour off any surplus solution, but do not replace the drainage hole plugs for a day or two, until the aggregate has had a chance to become thoroughly aerated again. Another method is to put buckets or jugs full of nutrient solution near the hydroponic units, with long pieces of wick or twisted cloth dipping into them. The other ends of these devices should be inserted a couple of inches into the growing medium in the pots or troughs. Liquid plant food will move along the wicks into the aggregate by capillary attraction, keeping it moist and affording nourishment to the plants for a reasonable time. There are now a number of automatic watering and solution applying devices produced by makers of horticultural equipment on the market, which can be utilised to solve the problem of prolonged absence if you wish to invest in such apparatus.

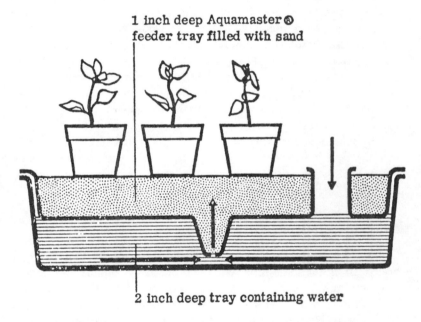

1 inch deep Aquamaster ® feeder tray filled with sand

2 inch deep tray containing water

FIG. 14 One type of proprietary automatic watering device.

To sum up: the simple hydroponic unit for home soilless gardening provides the means by which attractive blooms and health-giving vegetables, far superior to stale shop-bought ones, can be cultured by amateur gardeners and housewives at low cost, without any hard work, all the year round. Basically, the containers consist of supports in which the roots are anchored. These, combined with adequate but not excessive moisture, and inorganic feeding with mineral salts, supply a straightforward and technically balanced method of high quality home growing. It is all very much easier than soil cultivation, with its attendant dirt, laborious toil, and very likely disease-carrying manures. And it is also simple to set up, even in the smallest of dwelling places. The routine jobs of the hydroponicist are very light. The following points are the main ones to watch in daily care of units—

(a) Condition of the growing medium, including moisture content, any waterlogging, proper functioning of drainage holes, correct aeration and overheating or cold.

(b) Appearance of the plants. Any pests or diseases, proper tying and spacing, dirt or dust on foliage, satisfactory flower or fruit formation.

(c) Containers functioning properly.

(d) Environmental conditions, such as temperature, humidity, water and solution supply, light, shade, protection from wind and frost or rain.

(e) General, covering slow growth, fumes or gas, ventilation, hygiene, other errors or mistakes.

(f) Efficient application of nutrient solution.

CHAPTER VI

Keeping Plants Healthy

Hydroponic home garden units seldom give trouble when operated according to the simple method recommended and your soillessly grown plants will remain healthy if you follow the easy rules laid down and take normal precautions. Try to satisfy the needs of each lot of plants. Spend a few minutes daily looking them over, watch the leaves, stems, flowers and fruits for any warning signs and remember that love and care are vital. Hydroponics is a scientfic and controlled system of growing, but, as in all such activities, when we are dealing with living organisms, a little human interest will be well rewarded.

IF TROUBLE COMES

The first thing to do is to prepare a check list covering such items as light, air, moisture in the aggregate, fumes, situation, hygiene and other significant points. Go through this, noting any likely causes. Light deficiency can give rise to poor blooms, weak stems, often elongated, and very pale leaves—a condition known as *chlorosis*. Sudden collapse may be caused by noxious gases or smoke and fumes. The leaves are excellent indicators of a plant's state of health. Leaf drop can be started by several things—overwatering, too dry an aggregate, or very sudden changes in temperature are some of the reasons for this trouble. Yellow or drooping leaves are frequently traceable to an excessively wet growing medium, with the drainage holes not being opened regularly or failure to feed properly with nutrient solution. Black leaves are dead, and frost and sun scald may be the culprits, while browning of the tips often arises from overfeeding (that is, not using the correct amounts of the nutrient formula in the water), exposure to draughts, and possibly too much liquid standing around the crown of the plant where roots and stem join. Leaf spotting is commonly ascribed to sun scald or watering from above in strong sunshine. Rotted stems come from too wet roots and over-application of solution. Stunted growth with small leaves, a halt in development and lack of bloom on flowering plants can be attributed to inadequate nutrition and light, or failure to look after particular needs of different types of plants. A common cause of trouble with household plants is lack of humidity in the atmosphere.

Do not try to treat complaints by applying all suggested cures at once; use your check list to eliminate the various possibilities in turn and endeavour to test each remedy in succession until you find the exact problem and its answer.

DISEASES AND PESTS

Neglected plants frequently fall victim to diseases and pests far more easily than do those that are vigorous and well cared for. Provided the simple instructions given in this book are followed and the hydroponic unit set up properly, soilless gardening for the home is remarkably free from the diseases that beset soil cultivation. Remember, though, not to import disease organisms by sowing contaminated or doubtful seeds in your containers or by buying seedlings grown in soil from nurseries and shops and planting them, unwashed, in your soilless unit. That is asking for trouble.

Diseases such as rot and mildew or other fungus infections are generally encouraged by overwatering or using excess quantities of solution and by too damp conditions, lack of ventilation and overcrowding. Good hygiene and proper regulation of the environment are the best preventives. Various fungicides are available for spraying plants that are attacked.

The most widespread pests include ants, aphids or greenfly, caterpillars, mealybugs, red spider mites, scale insects, thrips, and white fly. A number of insecticides recommended for destroying these nuisances are readily available from garden centres, chemists' shops and other stores. Liquid derris and pyrethrum-based sprays are effective and quite safe to use in the home or garden, but always cover fish tanks or bowls in the vicinity before applying insecticides. For scale insects and mealybugs, however, treat by rubbing them off gently with a matchstick tipped with cottonwool soaked in methylated spirits, if time permits. Ant repellents may be bought easily. Normally, in clean surroundings, the incidence of insect pests will be very much less than in places where rubbish is allowed to accumulate or where dirty conditions prevail.

Sometimes, a slight greening of the surface of the aggregate in the hydroponic containers may occur, indicating the presence of algae. To check this, water occasionally with a solution made up of 0·5 of a gramme of copper sulphate dissolved in two gallons of water, or pro rata. If the trouble is extensive repeated waterings may be given every two or three days until the algae disappear. Copper sulphate may be obtained and weighed out at any good chemist. Algae infection normally arises mainly when conditions are rather damp.

AVOIDING ERRORS

Prevention is always better than cure. Experience over many years shows that failures in hydroponcs occur most frequently because the growing instructions have not been followed. So please bear in mind that you are operating a scientific and controlled method of plant culture. Simple indeed it is, and perhaps because of this you may be tempted to occasionally forget the few straightforward rules. For plants in household and amateur hydroponic gardens, the chief points never to be forgotten are:

(a) Always see that the aggregate in the containers is as moist as a damp sponge that has been wrung out lightly. Do not over-irrigate the growing medium or let it get too dry, and open the drainage holes periodically to give aeration.

(b) Give the particular plants you are growing the best environment and conditions that you can, so that their needs for light, ventilation, warmth, and other physical requirements are met as far as may be practicable.

(c) Follow the mixing up instructions for the nutrient formula you choose and for the preparation of the solution of plant food most carefully. Be sure to use the right quantities of the fertiliser mixture to the stated amounts of water. Don't guess at these and remember to apply the solution regularly, as the season demands, according to the crops' needs, to keep the aggregate moist and the plants vigorous and healthy. There is nothing complicated about this and a few days' experience will show you just how much solution will bring the growing medium to a nice degree of moisture and maintain it there at different times.

(d) Maintain strict hygiene: in technical terms we call this proper phytosanitary precautions. Be a keen observer and get to know each group of plants. Your care and patient attention will be well repaid.

CHAPTER VII

Flowers for the Home

Soilless gardening is a hobby that combines both science and art, affording ample scope for ingenious and attractive arrangements and floral displays. With hydroponics you can be sure of good technical control over plants. Beginners will find home growing without soil can bring much satisfaction and many interesting and happy hours spent in the operation of hydroponic units. All the same, home gardeners succeed best when they develop an awareness of the needs and habits of different kinds of plants. There is no real substitute for abundant and loving care and an observant mind. Today, most householders, given space, will also be amateur gardeners. The value of soilless culture is that, even when conditions are congested, the chance of having a garden, small though it may be, is not lost. New fashions in flowers have appeared, with varieties for contrasting requirements. Year by year, the popularity of home-grown blooms increases.

The urge to have flowers and foliage in and around homes is very old. The Romans grew plants in pots in their villas, and, for centuries both the Japanese and the Chinese have specialised in miniature indoor gardens, as well as larger outside ones. In Europe, covered orangeries were once a feature of stately houses, while cottages and town residence windows used to be bright with fuschias and geraniums in summer time. Many tropical lands are well known for the beautiful plant houses attached to the homes of important people. Still, numerous amateurs and housewives continue to suffer grievous disappointments in their efforts to grow garden flowers and indoor plants. Millions of plants die quickly owing to the failure of their owners to look after them properly or because of wrong cultural advice. Then, too, most specimens bought from stores, nurseries, florists and markets have been forced into unnatural development by artificial means before sale, or may be infected with diseases not apparent to the untrained eye at the time of purchase. The soils or composts in which they are rooted are frequently unsuitable or rapidly become exhausted. Consequently, such plants soon languish and die.

It is partly to avoid such misfortunes and losses that the new easy-to-use hydroponic method discussed in this book has been devised, while the simple growing techniques will provide a reliable means of starting the beginner on the right lines.

CHOOSING FLOWERS

The first thing to do is to decide exactly why you want each lot of plants. Very many types of house and garden flowers have been grown successfully in hydroponics. Perhaps the greatest amount of work has been carried out with carnations and chrysanthemums—often for commercial purposes. While much depends on local conditions, including things like temperature, light and humidity, there is normally no problem in raising all kinds of flowers in properly run soilless gardens. Flowers are usually grouped into the following categories.

(a) *Alpines* Strictly speaking, plants from mountainous regions, but loosely used to refer to all dwarf types suitable for rock gardens. They may be hardy herbaceous perennials, biennials, annuals, or shrubs.

(b) *Annuals (Half-hardy)* These complete their cycle of growth in one year, but need protection from cold in certain regions during spring time.

(c) *Annuals (Hardy)* These are resistant to cold.

(d) *Aquatics* Plants that grow wholly or mainly in water.

(e) *Bedding plants* This is a garden term only, having no botanical significance. It refers to those ornamentals that can be used for massed effects.

(f) *Biennials* Plants which complete their cycle of life in two years. They do not normally flower in the first year.

(g) *Bulbs* There are hardy and half-hardy bulbs as well as tender kinds.

(h) *Herbaceous perennials* Plants that live for a number of years and have a comparatively soft growth. They may be hardy or tender.

(i) *Epiphytes* Plants that may grow on other plants without being parasitic.

(j) *Shrubs and climbers*
(k) *Roses*
(l) *Miscellaneous types* Including flowering and decorative herbs for scent.

Here are a few notes about some attractive species for growing in hydroponic units, whether in the home, in greenhouses and conservatories, or outside in beds and troughs for the house garden.

Antirrhinums (Snapdragons)

The seeds may be sown in a tray of sand and the young plants later removed to their permanent positions with a ball of sand intact around their roots. Antirrhinums like generous treatment. It is a good plan to pinch out the tops when the seedlings are a few inches high, this discourages too early flowering and results in better root growth with more blooms eventually.

Asters

Moderate shading is beneficial. Checks in growth should be avoided, but no great differences have been observed in plants moved with a ball of sand around their roots and those transplanted with washed and clean roots, as far as ultimate development is concerned. Violent temperature fluctuations are undesirable. The plants are gross feeders and will need plenty of nutrient solution at all times.

Begonias

These plants have low light tolerance and need protection from direct sunshine. An air temperature of between 70° and 80° F is ideal. The growing medium should be on the moister side, but not too wet. When grown from seeds, begonias need considerable care and attention for the first few weeks. It is preferable to sow the seeds in pans of sand or vermiculite and cover them with a sheet of glass. Do not apply water or solution from the top but push a wick through the drainage hole, dipping the other end into a vessel of nutrient solution. The liquid will pass into the aggregate by capillary attraction, keeping it moist. Alternatively, stand the pan on a shallow tray with some solution in it.

Calceolarias

These beautiful and elegant flowers must be protected from

damage by wind and rain. Shading is necessary in very hot weather. Calceolarias are easy to grow in hydroponics, provided you give them warmth in cold periods.

Cannas

Often called Indian Shot, these flowers are the tropical gardener's stand-by. The seeds are very hard and should be filed or treated by scalding with boiling water before sowing, otherwise germination will be very slow. The plants can, however, be multiplied readily by root division. Cannas are gross feeders, requiring plenty of nutrient solution.

Carnations

Carnations are very well adapted to hydroponics, being grown extensively on a commercial scale in many lands. The plants need ample supplies of nutrient solution and are susceptible to extremes in temperature, overwatering and irregular irrigations. These errors should be avoided when growing the plants. After the flowers have been cut, you will find that you can improve their keeping qualities considerably by standing them in a solution of one part of boric acid powder and ten parts of water. Boric acid powder or crystals may be obtained from any chemist.

Chrysanthemums

Good drainage is essential, and as long as aeration is correct, top results should be secured. Propagation is normally by cuttings rooted in trays filled with moist sand or vermiculite, but seed can also be used with the Cascade varieties. Pinching out of the growing tips, or 'stopping', is essential to first-class production of flowers. Tables of the correct stopping dates for the different varieties of chrysanthemums are available in most books on these plants.

Dahlias

Dahlias need a well moistened aggregate, with satisfactory aeration and drainage. The plants are tender and most suceptible to frost injury. Propagation is by cuttings rooted in sand or vermiculite trays, or by root division. Dahlias do well in soilless garden units, but care must be taken to see that mildew does not occur, due sometimes to weakness caused by over-stimulation.

Gardenias
To get the best growth from gardenias, the water supply should not be too alkaline or hard. The plants like a humid atmosphere with ample irrigation. Propagation is normally by cuttings started in trays full of sand.

Gladioli
The plants are easy to grow and respond well to care and attention. Good lighting is essential.

Iris
This species grows excellently in hydroponics, but may be liable to decay in the rhizomes if over-watered. In areas of high humidity, iris should be planted close to the surface of the aggregate, but in hot, dry places an inch or two lower down will be best.

Marigolds
These plants are of different types, but all need good aeration. Some of the French species may like a finer growing medium and more moisture than do the African kinds.

Narcissi (Daffodils)
Bulbs should be planted at a depth equal to about three times their own thickness.

Nasturtiums
These flowers are very simple to grow, needing chiefly an ample supply of light and sunshine, with good aeration. They can be planted in hanging baskets or containers for balcony or verandah decoration.

Pansy
Pansies demand good irrigation and plenty of nutrient solution. Shade is desirable and they are not well suited to very dry places, unless kept fairly damp. When moving pansy seedlings, a good ball of sand or aggregate should always be kept around their roots.

Pelargoniums
These like a coarser aggregate, with very good aeration of the roots. A dry atmosphere is best, with adequate feeding and reason-

able shelter from the elements. The cuttings of pelargoniums or geraniums can be rooted easily in sand or vermiculite.

Petunias

Seeds are small and need great care for successful germination. Over-watering should be avoided. The plants are well suited to growing in small boxes or troughs in the hydroponic unit, on account of their natural drooping configuration.

Roses

Proper aeration and drainage are vital to good rose development in soilless gardens. Light intensity should be good, but sun scorch is undesirable. The best temperatures are from 60° to 80° F, though the range of tolerance is quite wide. The rose was the first ornamental plant to be grown in hydroponics by Dr W. F. Gericke in California. Roses are probably more sensitive to the effects of environment than most other plants and each situation should be judged separately when contemplating growing the flowers. Regular pruning is necessary. Strong growths should be cut down to within three dormant buds of the surface of the aggregate, weaker ones to within one or two buds, and very thin shoots should be removed altogether. Propagation is by cuttings, budding, and sometimes seeding.

Stocks

These plants present no particular difficulties in hydroponics, but they will not usually withstand temperatures of over 75° F. They are fairly tolerant of moisture and a damp atmosphere. Seed can be sown in trays of sand or fine aggregate and the young plants subsequently removed to their permanent containers.

Sweet Peas

Direct seeding is the best and the aggregate should be kept cool and moist, with overhead shading if the area is hot and dry. The seeds may be sown at a depth of as much as an inch below the surface of the growing medium. Care must be taken when applying nutrient solution to the containers, since too much wetness will cause rotting, while excessive dryness will result in desiccation. Hence the vital need to maintain moderately moist conditions. As the plants develop, more light and air must be given, so long as the temperature around the root zone does not rise unduly. If there is any trouble with overheating of the aggregate a cooling mulch of damp newspaper may be placed over the trough or bed surface during very warm periods, removing it at nights.

Zinnias

These flowers are very tolerant of high light intensities and can withstand considerable heat. Zinnias are gross feeders, needing plenty of nutrient solution.

INDOOR DECORATION

The demand for flowering and foliage plants for growing inside the home has increased greatly in recent years. Perhaps you may like to decorate halls and rooms, to flank doorways, brighten up windows or screen uninteresting views. Or do you just wish to live with beautiful flowers and refreshing greenery? Try to match the choice of plants as far as possible to the conditions in which you live and the place or position in which they will grow, making sure that they meet your needs and you like the types or styles.

Plants for inside the home are often classified as upright, bushy, squat, trailing or climbing in shape. Some of them live for years; many flower only for a season or two and then require replacing. Again, you may like coloured leaves or variegated and brightly tinted foliage. Fashions alter and some people want to be 'with it' in selecting novel and currently popular kinds. Of course, plants differ in their stamina—there are robust species and delicate species. Remember also that such details as the amount of light and sunshine available, the dryness or humidity of particular rooms and situations, the amount of space, together with the time you can spare to keep a check on your garden, are significant. Conditions can vary considerably in houses. Certain rooms may be shady and cool, others light but without any direct sunshine during part or whole of the day or lacking the advantage of good windows. Factors such as no heat in winter, old-fashioned gas fires, dampness, draughts, and a very dry atmosphere can affect plant growth markedly. Although household plants can tolerate quite a lot of adversity, the best results will be secured if you select types suited to your particular environment or try to make the conditions fit the basic needs of the ones you choose. In hydroponics, the cultural side of plant growth is well taken care of by the scientifically planned method of operation but it is still necessary to watch these other points.

Within the classes of plants for decoration already mentioned, inside the home, there is a wide range of types from which to choose. Thus we have flowering house and pot species, some capable of living indefinitely and others that last for a period of time only. Foliage household plants are noted for the attractiveness of their leaves and general form, while bulbs and corms usually provide splashes of colour for a few weeks at various seasons. Cacti and succulents and miniature trees can exist for years, as long as their needs are met. Then there are a large number of miscellaneous varieties, including various lovely annuals, different floral perennials, flowering herbs, plants grown from pips and stones, and greenery produced from cut roots.

Some suggestions for indoor hydroponic units, to give decorative effects, could include—

Indoor Flowers and House Plants

NAME	REMARKS
Achimenes (Cupid's Bower)	Usually summer flowering
Adiantum (Maidenhair Fern)	Needs moist and pure air
Aechmea (Urn Plant)	Long lasting
Aglaonema (Chinese Evergreen)	Dislikes fluctuations in winter temperatures
Anthurium (Flamingo Plant)	Lasts a few months
Antirrhinum (Snapdragon)	
Aphelandra (Zebra Plant)	
Araucaria (Norfolk Island Pine)	Well suited to pots
Asparagus (Asparagus Fern or Sparrow Grass)	Easy to grow
Aspidistra (Cast Iron Plant)	Very tolerant of conditions
Azalea	Dislikes draughts. Flowering often depends on house temperatures
Begonia	By careful choice of different types, it is possible to secure begonias in flower almost all the year round

Beloperone (Shrimp Plant)

Billbergia

Bougainvillea — Needs good light and warmth

Bulbs — Narcissus, daffodil, Roman hyacinth, crocus hyacinth, muscari, iris, snowdrop, lilies, Glory of the Snow, freesia, tulip, arum or calla, vallota, squill, gladioli, amaryllis, among others

Cacti — Many species, of which some interesting ones are: *Aloe variegata*, lithops, *Chamaecereus silvestrii*, *Echeveria retusa*, echinocactus, *Epiphyllum hybridum*, *Kalanchoe blossfeldiani*, *Mammillaria boscasana*, *Opuntia microdasys*, and *Zygocactus truncatus*

Calceolaria (Slipper Flower) — Does not like direct sunlight and prefers airy conditions

Calendula (Pot Marigold)

Camellia

Campanula (Italian Bellflower) — Trailing plant

Celosia (Cockscomb or Prince of Wales' Feathers) — Half-hardy, will flower during all the winter

Chrysanthemum — Selection of different varieties will ensure year-round blooming

Cineraria — Flowers in winter and spring

Cissus (Kangaroo Vine) — Dislikes draughts

Citrus (Sweet Orange) — Dwarf lemons, citrons and grapefruits also make attractive house plants

Clivia (Kaffir Lily) — Quite adaptable in rooms

Codiaeum (Croton) — Needs warmth, moist air and constant temperature

Coleus (Flame Nettle)

Columnea — Needs constant warmth and moisture

Crossandra

Cyclamen (Sowbread) — Blooms in winter time

Cyperus (Umbrella Plant) — Likes moist and cool conditions

Dianthus (Carnations, Pinks)

Dieffenbachia (Dumb Cane) — Needs warmth and moist air

Dizygotheca (False Aralia) — Requires warmth and moist air

Dracaena (Dragon Plant) — Warmth and moisture necessary

Drosera (Sundew) — Insectivorous plant

Erica (Cape Heath) — Flowers in winter and spring and requires freedom from draughts and moist air

Fatshedera (Fat Headed Lizzie)

Fatsia (Japanese Aralia or Castor Oil Plant)

Ferns — A wide variety. Popular types are: nephrolepis, pellaea, polypodium, pteris

Ficus (Fig, Rubber Plant) — Draughts cause leaf yellowing, strong sun not liked

Fuchsia (Lady's Eardrops)

Genista (Broom) — Cool, well-lit and airy rooms provide the best growing conditions

Geranium (Crane's Bill)

Gloxinia — Needs warmth and moist air

Grevillea (Silk Oak) — Dwarf. Likes cooler conditions

Hedera (Ivy) — Requires some moist air but generally neither strong light or warmth

Helxina (Mind Your Own Business) — Easy to grow, needs roots keeping moist

Herbs	Sweet basil, chives, dill, lavender, lemon balm, lemon geranium, verbena, lovage, majoram, mint, parsley, rosemary, sage, savory, tarragon, thyme, balsam, woodruff, and fennel will all thrive in soilless home garden units
Hibiscus (Chinese Rose)	Likes well-lit places
Hoya (Wax Plant)	Needs warmth and moisture
Hydrangea	To improve the blue colour of the flowers, water at intervals with a solution of aluminium sulphate (3 ozs to a gallon of water)
Impatiens (Busy Lizzie)	
Ipomoea (Moonflower, Morning Glory)	A climbing type
Jasminium (Jasmine)	
Lantana (Surinam Tea Plant)	
Maranta (Prayer Plant)	Adaptable, likes light, cool and airy places
Mimosa (Sensitive Plant)	Easy to grow
Monstera (Swiss Cheese Plant)	Aerial roots hanging from stem
Neanthe (Dwarf Palm)	Unsuitable for full sun, needs slightly humid conditions. Best palm for ordinary rooms
Nerium (Oleander)	Needs ample irrigation. Poisonous, so care is needed where there are children
Nidularium (Bird's Nest)	
Orchids	Good results in rooms may be secured with cymbidium, coelogyne, and cypripedium
Oxalis (Cape Shamrock or Wood Sorrel)	Suited to hanging pots

Pandanus (Screw Pine)	Needs warm and moist conditions
Passiflora (Passion Flower)	Sun essential
Pelargonium (Common geranium)	Light airy position best, no draughts and protection from frost. Series of plants can be grown for year-round flowering
Peperomia (Pepper Elder)	
Philodendron	Prefers shady conditions
Pilea (Aluminium Plant)	Fairly tolerant, but dislikes draughts
Poinsettia	Winter flowering, needs moist air and freedom from draughts
Polyanthus	
Primula	Several species. Long flowering periods, so stocks of primulas may be grown all the year
Rhoeo (Boat Lily)	
Rhoicissus (Grape Ivy)	Likes good light and ample moisture
Rosa (Roses)	Allow good light. Dwarf
Saintpaulia (African Violet)	Needs moist still air
Sansevieria (Mother-in-Law's Tongue)	Very tolerant of dry atmosphere. Should not be over-moistened
Saxifraga (Mother of Thousands)	Easy to grow. Wall display
Scindapsus (Ivy Arum)	Climber
Solanum (Winter Cherry)	Needs moist and cool atmosphere
Sparmannia (African Hemp)	
Spathiphyllum (Peace Lily)	Requires moist air. Long lasting
Spiraea (Astilbe)	
Streptocarpus (Cape Primrose)	Needs shading from strong sunshine

Tagetes (African and French Marigolds)	
Tetrastigma (Chestnut Vine)	Vigorous and good for screening
Thunbergia	Hanging or wall display
Tolmiea (Pickaback Plant)	Dislikes too bright light
Tradescantia (Spiderwort)	A trailing plant
Tropaeolum (Nasturtium)	Edible foliage for salads
Viola (Pansy)	Tolerates shady conditions, if not too damp
Vriesia	Requires good light
Zebrina (Wandering Jew)	
Zinnia	Easy to grow

Note: This list is not, of course, in any way exhaustive. Many other attractive plants are available for indoor soilless gardening. Most popular annuals, of which there are seeds available in stores, will add vivid splashes of colour to the home.

THE ART OF ARRANGEMENT

Plants bring into our homes a breath of life and great natural beauty. During dull winter months, their gay colours cheer us up, while on hot summer days the green foliage and delicate blossoms look cool and refreshing. With a little imagination, very charming and tasteful interior decorations may be achieved with floral displays. A wide variety of arrangements for growing hydroponic flowers indoors, in backyards, greenhouses, or in the garden area, as well as house plants, are easy to devise with little trouble or effort. Here are some interesting ideas for soilless home gardeners.

Troughs and pots

Ready-made troughs and pots of different lengths or sizes can be bought at garden shops, department stores, or other suppliers. It is best to choose stone, pottery, or plastic types, although wooden boxes and containers are suitable if you line them with polythene sheeting. If metal kinds are used, be sure that they are painted inside with a non-toxic paint, emulsion or varnish. This is particularly important in the case of galvanised iron troughs and receptacles. Decorative specimens are termed *jardinières*. For most plants grown in home hydroponic units or soilless gardens, troughs and pots should be about six inches deep—to allow ample space for rooting.

FIG. 15 Ready made troughs and pots, with stands, suitable for hydroponics.

To make pots more attractive you can get hiders of fancy wire, cane, pottery, or coloured plastic or you can even use copper bowls and small buckets. Single pots standing by themselves should have saucers placed underneath to catch seepage when the drainage holes are opened. In the case of troughs, one or two tin lids or a shallow tray will do the same job. Often containers of pleasing designs can be bought with attached legs and others can be set up on stands to suit individual wishes. It is also very simple to make your own hydroponic receptacles at home, using wooden boxes, roofing felt or polythene sheeting stretched over frames, or asbestos, while in the greenhouse or outside garden, beds and troughs of bricks and

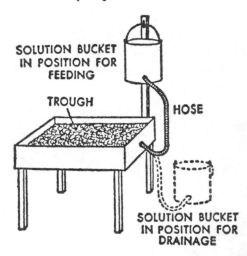

SOLUTION BUCKET
IN POSITION FOR
FEEDING

TROUGH

HOSE

SOLUTION BUCKET
IN POSITION FOR
DRAINAGE

FIG. 16 A portable household trough with semi-automatic feeding and drainage. This is useful for moving from place to place as required.

mortar, concrete and other available materials can be constructed in whatever positions appeal to you. By fixing buckets or tanks to upright posts or placing them just above containers, so that they can be raised and lowered as desired, a semi-automatic way of applying the nutrient solution is easy to arrange.

Window Boxes

Several alternative methods of using window boxes or troughs are practicable. In summer, the containers can be put out on the sills. At other seasons, it is best to have them on ledges inside, where adequate light is available, while the glass panes afford protection from cold and frost. Especially delightful are hydroponic plant windows, with long troughs running across the full width of picture-windows. These heighten the effect of the area of glass and break up its monotony. Venetian blinds can be employed to exclude sun scorch or excessive cold. Climbing displays are also useful for framing windows.

Tiers

All sorts of tiered hydroponic arrangements can add enjoyment to home hydroponic gardening. For example, shelving or staging, with various containers distributed at appropriate intervals, will provide screens, room dividers, door framers, and similar decors. There must be enough space left between tiers to allow plants to grow to their desirable heights.

Wall displays

Special wall-mounted containers may be obtained and these usually include a drainage saucer. These look good in halls, corridors or along staircases, as well as in rooms or beside windows.

Terrariums

These are smaller self-contained groupings, enclosed in carboys, large bottles, globes, fish bowls or tanks, and even big drinking glasses.

FIG. 17   A Terrarium.   A Hanging Basket.

Miniatures

Generally, bowls are employed, with reproductions of Lilliputian or small-scale garden models, including suitable plants and toy summerhouses, pagodas, bridges, or windmills, together with paths and related embellishments. Rather similar are *indoor groups* of plants growing in a single container, combining tall and shorter specimens.

Other suggestions

Some people are very fond of bark and log arrangements consisting of attractively positioned stumps or cut branches and suitable plants. The *pot-et-fleur* containers are mixed indoor groups, with tubes inserted at intervals in the growing medium to hold cut flowers in place, which can be renewed or changed from time to time to provide variety and extra brilliance.

Hanging baskets are normally made from wire and are lined with moss, in which a bowl or pot is put to act as the plant growth container. For climbing plants, pendant strings or chains or light canes will give support and it is also possible to set up a trellis. Herbs do well in pans, especially being suited to the kitchen or pantry, while fruit pips and stones placed in pots will develop into tiny trees of fascinating appearance. Dwarf or miniature trees, produced by the Japanese art called *bonzai*, and trained into shape by

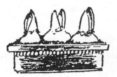

FIG. 18   Bulbs.

cutting, pinching and wiring, are becoming increasingly popular, but the process of culture is a lengthy one. Bulbs thrive in saucers filled with damp aggregate. The cut-off tops of carrots, turnips, beetroots and parsnips, planted in shallow containers, will soon give rise to fern-like masses of feathery fronds, useful for background greenery. Pineapple tops may similarly be cultured without trouble. Indeed, the enterprising amateur gardener or householder should have no difficulty in thinking up all sorts of interesting and conventional floral and foliage arrangements for indoor hydroponics.

CHAPTER VIII

Vegetables and Salads for the Kitchen

The word vegetable is derived from the Latin term *vegetabilis*, meaning animating. Fresh greenfood is an essential constituent of all balanced diets. The importance of vegetables and fruits for the maintenance of good health and bodily vigour is generally recognised today. During recent years, the popularity of the salad vegetables has increased steadily, so that now there will be few households in which tomatoes, lettuces, cucumbers or other fresh produce of similar type do not find a place. Correspondingly, the interest in the basic greenstuffs, such as cabbages, spinach, brussels sprouts, green beans, and cauliflowers, as well as in aubergines, sweet peppers and other more exotic produce, has also risen, since, once accustomed to the taste of fresh vegetables, people are loath to do without them in some form or other at times when perhaps their first choices may be unavailable. In home hydroponic gardens you can grow all the vegetables and salads you may desire, together with some fruits and root crops or potatoes, if you wish. The exact selection of the plants will of course depend upon the personal preferences of the housewife or amateur gardener and the space available. Local climatic conditions and facilities for giving protection during periods of colder weather are further factors that have to be taken into account. But it is worth remembering that hydroponic vegetables and fruits mature more quickly than those planted in soil, produce far higher yields and need less space.

RECOMMENDED CROPS

In 1947, Mr T. Eastwood, then active in international hydroponic work, recommended the following list of vegetable crops as very well suited to household soilless gardening:

Tomatoes, green beans, cucumber, aubergine or egg-plant, sweet peppers (chillies), radish, green or spring onions, lettuces, turnip greens, mustard greens, Chinese cabbage greens, Swiss chard, celery, and spinach.

Of course, we can grow many more and this list only mentions a few types that are extremely simple to cultivate hydroponically. Before going on to discuss these kinds of vegetables, and others as well, in further detail, there are three points about cropping in soil-less gardens that are worth remembering. First of all, you can take advantage of what is called intercropping. Some plants take up more space with their foliage or leaves than with their roots, thus leaving a free area of aggregate at surface level. Between such tall plants, lines of smaller specimens that appreciate a little shade may be sown or intercropped. Examples are lettuces between rows of tomato plants, radishes among peas, and endive interspersed with French or runner beans. Then there is catch cropping. This means that while larger plants are developing, seeds of quicker growing catch crops may be sown in the troughs or containers. These latter will be ready for harvesting before the former need the extra room. Examples include salad greens planted among beetroots, dwarf beans with cabbages or mustard, and cress with celery. Finally, crops of different habits can be grown together in the same trough or bed with success, so saving an appreciable amount of space. Pumpkins or vegetable marrows and maize (sweet corn), tomatoes and new potatoes, or climbing beans and various root vegetables such as carrots, lend themselves to this combination.

Here is a list of the main vegetable crops, with some notes on looking after them:

Artichokes (Globe or French)

This is a perennial vegetable, which continues to reproduce for several years without replanting. Artichokes like good moisture but will not tolerate extremes of temperature. Protection from frost is necessary and shading in very hot weather. Cropping is most profitable in the second and third years.

Artichokes (Jerusalem)

This does well in hydroponics. As growth proceeds, a little extra aggregate should be drawn up towards the stems to make sure the tubers are properly covered. Some shade will be needed in very hot places.

Asparagus

Propagation is usually by seed, though crowns may be obtained for transplanting. As it does not begin to crop until the third year, catch sowings of lettuce or radish or some other salad vegetable should be sown between the rows until the space is needed by the asparagus. The plant is a gross feeder and requires plenty of nutrient solution. The growing medium should be fairly loose in texture and well aerated. For good white stems, blanching of the shoots is necessary. Plastic collars may be employed for this.

Aubergine (Egg-plant)

Garden eggs thrive best in a warm dry place. Plenty of nutrient solution will be needed and a moist aggregate should be always maintained. To secure the largest fruits, the points of growth may be reduced in number by pinching out. When fruit is forming, to prevent growth of leaves at the expense of the eggs, substitute plain water for nutrient solution every few days, returning to normal fertilising procedure when the fruits are well developed.

Beans

Many kinds of beans thrive in hydroponics, including broad, french, scarlet runner, lima, asparagus, velvet, soya and other types. The cultivation of beans is not difficult. Generally speaking, these crops demand good irrigation but should never be allowed to become waterlogged. Aeration of the roots is essential. Different species need different degrees of warmth.

Beetroot

Sowing can take place in trays of sand, the young seedlings being transplanted into the main containers when two to three inches high. As growth proceeds, a little extra aggregate should be placed around the roots. Beetroots are well adapted to hydroponics and their light requirements are moderate.

Brassicas

These include broccoli and cauliflowers, cabbages, brussel sprouts, pe-tsai or Chinese cabbage, red cabbage, kale, kohl-rabi and turnips. All belong to to the brassica group of vegetables. They are sensitive to lack of air in the growing medium, but need frequent applications of nutrient solution. The drainage of the hydroponic unit must be kept in good working order when brassicas are grown. Cabbages, in particular, are gross feeders. Cauliflowers do best when they are unchecked and can make heads quickly.

Carrots

Carrots need quite a lot of attention, but once the seedlings have taken hold good growth will result. The shorter varieties may penetrate better into the aggregate. Too coarse or heavy a growing medium is not desirable for this crop.

Celery

For ease of sowing, the seeds may be mixed with a filler of sand. The plants need a cool and partially shaded position and will require blanching before harvest.* This can be done by putting plastic collars on the stems. Good aeration is essential for celery production in hydroponics.

Chicory

Seed can be sown in small boxes filled with sand or vermiculite, later on transplanting into the permanent growing container as convenient. For forcing chicory, the pots or troughs may be covered with inverted flower-pots or trays, but a better method is to lift the crowns and trim off any side-roots. The crowns should then be stacked in small boxes filled with aggregate, up to a depth of an inch or two. The growing medium must be kept just moist with solution and the whole unit put in complete darkness at a temperature of between 55° and 60° F. When the shoots attain a height of about seven inches they may be cut off and used. It is important to ensure that the blanching is thorough.

Chillies (Sweet and Hot Peppers)

These need plenty of nutrient solution, but do not like a humid atmosphere. Light shading can be given in very warm areas. Care must also be taken to provide protection against strong winds. In cold regions, cultivation should be inside the home or in greenhouses.

---

* Self-blanching varieties of celery are now available, but like the new tomato hybrid strains the flavour may not always compare with the older, conventional types.

Cucumbers

Seeds may be grown in sand boxes or trays and the young seedlings transplanted later into the main troughs or pots, making sure that there is no check to growth. Some supports must be provided for the vines to climb up. The best day temperatures for cucumbers are generally 75° to 85° F and they will stand over 100° F. Direct seeding is also quite practicable. For proper development of female flowers, a programme of terminal bud pinching is needed, unless the new varieties are grown. Cucumbers have very high water and solution requirements, needing frequent irrigation, fairly high atmospheric humidity, shelter from wind, shading during bright periods, and good general care.

Endive

This salad vegetable is easy to grow in soilless home gardens, being very similar to lettuce. For blanching, draw the leaves together and tie them up, so as to exclude light from the heart of the plant, or else cover the endives with inverted flower-pots, adjusted so that the air goes under the bottom.

Leeks

These are gross feeders. They will need ample amounts of nutrient solution. The stems can be blanched by putting on plastic collars. To prevent leeks running to seed in very warm conditions, cut the tap root with a sharp knife.

Lettuces

Lettuces should be grown quickly without any checks being permitted during development. Seed may be sown in sand boxes and the young seedlings later transplanted to the main containers. They can also be sown directly. A filler of fine sand can be added to the small seeds to ensure better distribution. In hot places, lettuce plants need shading and the troughs should be kept fairly cool. It is also important to see that no waterlogging occurs or else the lower leaves will rot and the root crowns may be damaged. This salad is quite simple to raise in household hydroponic units.

Melons

The two main types are cantaloupes or musk melons and water melons. The former like hot dry conditions, with ample irrigation and are susceptible to high air humidity. It is a good plan to place a small collar of damp-excluding material around the base of the plant's stem to keep it dry during growth. Water melons also prefer dry and warm spots but are hardier than cantaloupes. Both types may need hand pollinating.

Okra (Lady's Fingers)

These vegetables demand plenty of nutrient solution, warm conditions, satisfactory drainage, and good aeration. Before sowing, the seeds should be soaked in water for forty-eight hours, to encourage better germination.

Onions

Onions need reasonably dry conditions. Dampness does not favour good development. Spring onions may be treated like other salads, but for mature onions it is best to stop any irrigation once they have attained full size and allow the tops to dry out. The bulbs can then be lifted for storage.

Parsnips

Because of their very long roots, parsnips will want deeper containers than most hydroponic crops. The plants tolerate cold and ordinary frosts. To prevent forking of the roots, collars of fine metal gauze, painted with emulsion or good quality paint, can be inserted into the growing medium around each plant. These will stop any branching of the roots and encourage them to grow straight down.

Peas

Both dwarf and tall types are available. Peas need good aeration, freedom from very humid conditions and proper supports. In dry places, ample amounts of nutrient solution will be necessary. Seed may be sown directly in the containers.

Potatoes

It is important to ensure that the tubers are provided with an adequate covering of aggregate, otherwise overheating in warm times and greening may occur. The plants can withstand hot conditions provided the root zone is kept cool. Good aeration and drainage are vital, but potatoes also need ample supplies of nutrient solution. To sow the seed tubers, simply make holes in the growing medium about three inches deep and drop in the potatoes, raking back the aggregate over them. In household hydroponics the main interest in cultivating this crop will be to obtain better tasting new potatoes.

Radishes

Radishes cannot be transplanted, but should be sown directly into the main troughs or pots, often as catch or intercrops. They are very quick growing. Good shading is necessary in hot areas, or the plants may bolt.

Rhubarb

After planting, the crowns should just appear on the surface of the aggregate. Ample nutrition is necessary for rhubarb. Forcing may be undertaken by covering with inverted barrels or boxes.

Spinach

This crop needs ample applications of nutrient solution and a cool, shady site. There are several kinds of spinach, but all are normally fairly quick maturing. Seed may be sown in trays of sand and subsequently transplanted to the main hydroponic containers.

Squashes

Both vegetable marrows and squashes can be sown in sand boxes and the young seedlings later moved to their permanent pots or troughs. The plants like warmth, but are often adversely affected by excessive moisture. A piece of flat stone or tile should be placed under each fruit to prevent it from rotting. Hand pollination is often necessary for good fruiting. Squashes are one of the easiest vine crops to grow in hydroponics.

Sweet Corn

Maize seed can be sown directly in hydroponic containers, either alone or in combination with another crop. Ample solution may be applied. In warm positions, with shelter, but good light, sweet corn grows very rapidly. For table use, cobs should be picked fresh and lightly toasted, then spread with butter if desired. The sooner green corn is eaten the better, since it loses its full taste two hours after picking from the plant.

Sweet Potato

This crop needs a warm place with reasonably dry air conditions and shading from hot sun. It is a moderate feeder.

Tomatoes

Tomatoes should be protected from strong wind and excessive humidity. The plant likes warm conditions, some shading and proper aeration. Seed is best germinated in boxes or trays of sand and vermiculite, or other finer aggregates, and the young seedlings later moved to their permanent growing positions. The vines will require supports. Tomatoes become stunted if kept short of nutrient solution, so checks to growth should not be permitted. After the fourth truss, the main stem can be cut off and a side shoot taken on. This operation will restore pristine vigour to the plant. Suckers must be removed as they appear. The flowers of tomato plants can be syringed gently from time to time to encourage pollination, with better fruit formation. Tomatoes are probably the most widely grown vegetable crop amongst amateur hydroponicists.

Watercress

For the most effective growth of this crop the solution should be allowed to flow continuously from an elevated tank or bucket into the aggregate. As it passes out of the drainage holes, which are kept open all the time, it is collected in a sump or vessel and returned, at frequent intervals, to the overhead reservoir for recycling. Although seed is sometimes used, cuttings from selected plants give the best results. The temperature for watercress should be maintained at from 60° to 65° F. The rate of flow of the liquid should not be too quick; a speed of about one mile an hour is quite adequate.

Yams

Deeper beds will be necessary for this crop. Shading too, is essential. Care must be taken not to over-irrigate or the tubers will rot. The yam seed should be planted about ten inches below the surface of the growing medium and supports provided for the vines to climb on.

FRUITS

Strawberries are a popular hydroponic garden fruit crop. Runners are most suitable for starting in the troughs or beds in the soilless unit. They may either be forced for fruiting during the first season, or left in for three years, the best berries being then obtained in the second and third years. Much depends on the variety or type selected for growing. Care must be taken not to allow the plants to become waterlogged, nor should the leaves get saturated with nutrient solution or rot may set in.

Several other kinds of soft fruits can be grown in hydroponics. Very successful results have been secured with papayas or pawpaws, and pineapples which do well in greenhouses or conservatories. Grapes, also, thrive, given deep large pots.

RAPID GROWTH AND HIGH YIELDS

Vegetable crops mature earlier in soilless gardens than they do in soil. A sowing and planting programme for the household should take account of this fact so as to ensure that a continuous supply of fresh produce is available at all seasons. In Florida, growers obtain hydroponic tomatoes seventy days after planting seedlings. Californian experience shows that tomato fruits will be ready within sixty days or two months. Lettuces raised in hydroponics in England have produced good hearts a week or ten days earlier than similar sowings made in soil. French beans and radishes produced in United States Army soilless gardens took only thirty-five days to mature.

High yields are characteristic of hydroponics. With due care and proper growing conditions, your tomato plants can yield up to thirty pounds of fruit each. In commercial units it is common to get harvests of as much as two or three hundred tons per acre. Similar results have been secured with other crops.

Seeds vary greatly, according to variety and quality, in the time they take to germinate. Never buy doubtful seeds from unreliable firms—it is a waste of money. Always get fresh ones of guaranteed origin. Here are some average germination times for seeds in hydroponic home gardens:

Crop	Days
Beans, broad	7
Beans, french	9
Beans, runner	9
Beetroot	17
Beet seakale	17
Borecole	6
Broccoli	6
Brussels sprouts	6
Cabbages	6
Carrot	16
Cauliflower	6
Celery	17
Cress	4
Cucumber	5
Endive	12
Kale	6
Kohl-rabi	6
Leek	19
Lettuces	7
Mustard	4
Onion	10
Parsley	22
Parsnip	18
Peas	6
Radishes	5
Savoys	6
Spinach	8
Spinach beet	16
Swedes	6
Tomatoes	6
Turnip	6
Vegetable marrow	5

Different varieties may be quicker or slower to germinate, while temperature plays an important part in the length of time taken. The advice on seed packets should always be read carefully.

HERBS

These can be grown without difficulty in the kitchen, either on window ledges or by fixing up simple plastic tents just outside. If the tent is made from polythene sheets and designed in a lean-to style, it will be possible to allow hot air from the kitchen to flow through an open window or ventilator into the growing compartment, keeping it nice and warm in winter time. Suitable culinary species that do well in hydroponics include: borage, chervil, chives, fennel, garlic, horse-radish, marjoram, mint, parsley, rosemary, rue, sage, savory, tarragon, and thyme.

In growing hydroponic vegetables, salads, fruits and other edible plants in the home, the aim should be to secure as large a yield as quickly as possible from the smallest given area. With flowers, the object is frequently to obtain 'massed bank' effects. For foodstuffs, we normally like to have constant supplies and one way of achieving this is to sow a succession of crops, having another ready to use as soon as a previous and earlier lot is exhausted. Careful planning and a little forethought are all that are needed to get such results. As mentioned before, spacing between plants in hydroponics may be reduced, by as much as fifty per cent, as long as light availability is assured. This also assists in the production of higher yields from limited space.

CHAPTER IX

Miscellaneous Uses

Apart from the culture of flowers and vegetables, as well as fruits and herbs, for the home and household garden, there are a number of other ways in which hydroponics may come in handy for the family. In this chapter, several such uses are described and instructions given on their application.

GERMINATION NETS

Germination nets are quite useful for starting difficult seeds, which as they grow, may be moved in to the permanent containers. The method of construction consists of taking a piece of common cotton mosquito netting and dipping it into melted paraffin wax. Candles can be used for the purpose. While still as hot as possible the impregnated netting is tightly stretched over the top of an enamelware pan of convenient size and bound firmly beneath the marginal rim of the basin with a strong cord or string. The nutrient solution is then poured into the pan until the surface of the liquid comes into contact with the bottom of the net. The seeds, which have been previously soaked between pieces of damp blotting paper to make them swell, are now sprinkled on the treated net, where they soon develop, being in constant contact with the solution, yet freely exposed to the air. After they have attained a few inches in height they may be transferred to the pots or containers in the hydroponic garden.

INCREASING YOUR PLANTS

Although not everyone wants to propagate his or her own stock, other than seeds sown directly and then thinned out or transplanted, for those interested here is a short list of the possibilities of increasing your soilless garden plants by simple means.

Cuttings

These are easy to root in aggregate. Always ensure that stem cuttings are taken with a joint or node at the bottom. Remove the lower leaves and insert the stem half-way up into the growing medium. Stem, root, and leaf cuttings, as well as offsets are frequently used too, for certain plants. To assist root formation, rooting hormones may be bought from garden stores and big chemists.

Layering and division

To layer runners, simply peg them down at a convenient point half-an-inch into the aggregate. Roots will form in due course. Bulbs, ferns and some other types can be divided up to make more plants. Bulbs form tiny bulblets naturally, while root clumps may be separated with care. Afterwards, transplant the new specimens to their growing sites or containers.

Air-layering

This method is utilised for large ornamental plants or those difficult to root. Make a cut in the main stem, about two-thirds through it, and keep this open with a piece of matchstick. Wrap some moist sphagnum moss (available from garden stores or perhaps florists) around the open cut, enclose the whole in a piece of polythene sheeting and tie the ends to form a moisture-proof pack. When roots start to develop inside, cut off below the pack, remove this, and plant the top stem in another pot. New shoots will soon arise from the old stump.

Many home gardeners using hydroponics, prefer to sow their seeds separately in small boxes filled with sand or sand and aggregate mixture, later transplanting them into the permanent containers, when they are about two inches high. In soilless culture, removal is simple and there should be no check in growth. Cacti and succulents will do well in hydroponics, but always keep the aggregate rather drier than for other plants, and never over-irrigate with nutrient solution or you will get rotting of the stems and roots. Bulbs and corms, too, present no trouble; even a heap of moist aggregate on a saucer, regularly given solution, is adequate for them. Again, do not wet excessively and see that they get enough air. Fruit pips, planted like seeds, will often make pretty and interesting small household trees. Oranges, lemons, grapefruits, citrons, dates, apricots, avocado stones, and peaches are amongst the most easy to germinate. Remember also kitchen herbs, useful for culinary purposes, and for scent and small flowers or blossoms. Then there are root vegetable tops for greenery and similar miscellaneous attrac-

FIG. 19   Herbs.

tions. Rampion and dandelions, as well as corn salad, are quite useful at times and are well suited to household soilless gardening.

A WORD OF WARNING

If you are given, or buy, flowering plants or vegetable seedlings from nurseries, garden stores, or shops, rooted in soil or composts, never plant these directly in your hydroponic unit. To do so will cause serious risk of disease and upset the scientific balance of the soilless garden. Also, very often, such specimens have been forced under unnatural conditions and will soon die when taken into the home. If, however, you must have bought-in or gift plants, first treat them in the following way before putting them in your hydroponic unit.

Remove the plant from its pot, if it is in one, by up-ending it and place it with the soil still around its roots in a basin of clean water. Let it soak for a while until the earth or compost is freed from the roots. Transfer it gently to another basin, leaving the wet soil behind and repeat the process until the roots are quite bare and clean. Be careful not to treat it roughly or damage any roots. Then rinse them gently under a slowly running tap, to wash away any vestiges of soil or organic matter. When this has been done, dip the plant, roots and all, two or three times in a solution of water and formalin (Jeyes' Fluid), available from general stores or chemists' shops, prepared by adding one fluid ounce of the disinfectant to every two and a half to three pints of water. (There are twenty fluid ounces in a pint of water.)

After such treatment has been completed, put the plant straight into its new hydroponic container, arranging the roots carefully—not in one bunch, but spread out—and dribble the aggregate, previously moistened, with solution, around them. Continue until the plant is standing firmly in place and see that the growing medium holds it up nicely. Smooth over the surface and water well with the nutrient liquid. Keep quite moist, but well aerated for a while when it should have accustomed itself to its new surroundings, then treat it in the standard way. But there can be no guarantee that such bought-in shop plants will do as well as your own grown seedlings because of the forcing that they have undergone before sale. The same treatment can, of course, be applied to young seedlings or plants in boxes, germinated in soil or composts, and generally offered to the public in spring time.

VALUE IN TEACHING

For teaching and demonstration purposes in schools and colleges, hydroponic plants, growing in small portable units, are most useful. Children are fascinated by the science of soilless cultivation and really grasp the object of the system. Transparent plastic containers fitted with loose black paper covers to exclude light from the root zone are ideal for this work. On removing the covers in class, pupils may see development taking place. Hydroponics is a great aid in teaching botany, horticulture, agriculture or crop husbandry, plant physiology and rural science or nature study.

FLOATING RAFTS

If you have a pond or other stretch of water available, you can make hydroponic water gardens very cheaply. These are based on the floating gardens laid down by the Mogul emperors of India in Kashmir and the ancient *chinampa* of the Aztecs of Mexico. To make such a soilless garden, you need to build a small raft of light wood or similar material, pierced by a number of small holes. Cover this platform with a six-inch layer of light aggregate, with boards around the sides to keep the growing medium from falling off. Fit wicks through the holes in the bottom, passing from the water below into the aggregate. Sow or plant the chosen flowers in the aggregate, apply solution regularly, and rely for additional moisture on water moving by capillary action along the wicks. Periodic aeration is arranged by moving the raft or platform from time to time.

HANGING BASKETS

The hydroponic hanging basket consists of a trough or container which is slung from a system of overhead pulleys above a shallow basin full of nutrient solution. At regular intervals, the basket, which has a fine wire mesh base or else a number of inlet holes, to enable the nutrient solution to penetrate to the roots, is dipped into the liquid thus irrigating and feeding the plants growing in the container. A light aggregate mixture should be put in the wire mesh trough to anchor the plants' roots in position. A large hydroponic 'flower factory', growing mainly chrysanthemums for sale, is operated on this principle in North Carolina.

GREEN GRASS FOR PETS

Sprouting cabinets and household or stable hydroponic units for producing grass and fresh forage for your rabbits, guinea-pigs and other pets, as well as for horses and donkeys, are quite simple to set up. These are based on the soilless culture installations now employed by farmers to grow thousands of tons of greenfood for dairy cows and beef cattle. Some racehorse trainers also find the method valuable to provide thoroughbreds with a high quality diet throughout the year, especially when grazing is short in winter months.

To set up a home hydroponic grass growing unit you will require some shallow trays or troughs, about two or three inches deep and of any convenient length or width. These may be arranged in tiers or end to end. Inside each tray, place a thick piece of underfelting or layers of sacking. The medium must be kept moist with nutrient solution, made up to half-strength only. Take the grass seed or grains of oats, barley, or rye, and spread it fairly thickly over the medium in the tray, after having first soaked it overnight in a bowl of clean water. The damp seed or grain will germinate very quickly. Keep the unit in a semi-darkened room for a day or two or in a warm shed or stable, with good ventilation. When the tiny shoots reach the height of about half-an-inch, give them light, either natural or artificial. This will encourage a good green colour to develop. By maintaining such soilless grass growing outfits at a temperature of between 70° and 75° F it is possible to produce fresh green forage some seven to eight inches tall in a week or ten days. From

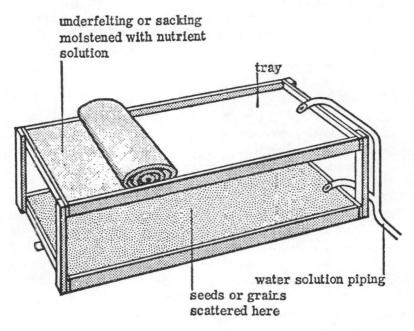

underfelting or sacking
moistened with nutrient
solution

tray

water solution piping

seeds or grains
scattered here

FIG. 20 Example of home hydroponic grass growing unit for producing fresh greenfood for pets.

time to time, add more nutrient solution until the fifth day, thereafter give only plain water and occasionally a gentle overhead spray to prevent drying out. Proper ventilation of the room or shed in which the hydroponic unit is situated is vital to first-class production. As soon as the grass or green forage is ready for harvesting peel off the 'mat' of food material and give it fresh to the pets or animals. You can then wash out the troughs or trays, clean the growing medium, replace it and sow again for another crop. To get daily output, have seven to ten trays, seed one every twenty-four hours, and harvest them in succession. If you wish, you may wash the grass before feeding it to the livestock, but by using only plain water for the last few days you will get very clean forage with no salt residues on it. The fertiliser formula helps add extra nutritional value to the grass. Pets of all kinds, as well as horses, love this fresh feed which helps them to keep healthy and fit, particularly in winter. It is also cheap to produce. More elaborate hydroponic grass-growing units of larger size can be built or bought ready made. Details of how to construct these will be found in more advanced literature or you can purchase them from J. A. Gordon & Son Ltd., Agricultural Engineers, Stonehouse, near Stroud, Gloucestershire, England.

ORCHIDS

To grow orchids, the best potting mixture is made up of equal parts of broken bricks, wood chippings, bark or shavings and sphagnum moss. For terrestial orchids, charcoal, small pieces of bone, and some coarse sand may be added. The plants are usually propagated by means of cuttings or divisions of the rootstock or pseudo-bulbs, although experts do raise them from seed. The germinating medium should be infected with the appropriate microscopic fungus mycelium, pure cultures of which are available. In the absence of the fungus, orchid seeds seldom germinate, or if they do, the seedlings will not thrive. Orchids should be given conditions which resemble those of the areas from which they originate, as far as temperature and humidity are concerned. This is normally done by growing them in greenhouses or conservatories.

OFFICE UNITS

The selection of plants for offices usually centres around tropical foliage types that will withstand high and fluctuating temperatures, low humidity and poorer light conditions. Three plants that are most tolerant of poor lighting, low humidity, or neglect are:

(i) Cast Iron Plant or *Aspidistra elatior,*
(ii) India Rubber Tree or *Ficus elastica,*
(iii) Mother-in-law's Tongue or *Sansevieria trifasciata.*

Aspidistras suffered a decline in popularity, but are now making quite a come-back, especially the variegated form with large ovate leaves on long petioles arising from ground level. The Rubber plant has ovate oblong leaves, formed on tall woody stems. The variegated types are the most attractive. The Snake plant, sometimes called Mother-in-Law's Tongue, is Indian in origin, not African, and has stiff spear-like leaves that stand erect from the surface of the growing medium. Here again, the modern variegated forms are pleasant, with intriguing crossbands of lighter and darker shades of green, or sometimes marginal bands of yellow, for a change.

Ficus or fig types can be very dependable and offer variety of leaf form. These include:

Fiddle-leaved fig or *Ficus lyrata*, with large fiddle-shaped leaves.
Weeping fig or *Ficus benjamina*, with willow-like wavy-margined leaves.
Java fig or *Ficus benjamina*, var. *exotica*, with a more refined and graceful form.
Mistletoe fig or *Ficus diversifolia*, which has distinctive, smaller, obovate leaves and is very well adapted to office planting. This type forms a twiggy plant, slow growing and able to withstand quite adverse conditions, particularly poor light.

The Umbrella trees or Scheffleras can thrive in more dry conditions than most other tropical species for office use. There are three kinds common, all with large palmately compound umbrella-like leaves. They need ample light, but will withstand less favoured situations quite well.

The Palm family: in very large offices, where graceful plants that will tolerate low light intensities and low humidity are desired, thought should be given to using members of the palm family. In these kinds of situations, the following should respond well.

Sentry palm or *Howea belmoreana*,
Paradise palm, or *Howea forsteriana*,
Neanthe palm or *Chamaedorea elegans* Bella possessing miniature proportions,
Large lady palm or *Rhapis excelsa*, a very hardy species, tolerant of abuse, with a bamboo-like appearance and fan-shaped leaves.

In lobbies or places where there is warmth, but also draughts, *Philodendron sellowianum* and *Philodendron hastatum*, are to be recommended. In really cool conditions, variegated ivies and aucubas are best and will probably suffice. Office plants should have their names written on labels attached to their containers. This adds greatly to their interest. Hydroponics is the ideal system for growing decorative plants in offices, stations, public buildings, and other such places. It is worth mentioning that automatic methods of soilless gardening have become popular for installation in large offices. Mr Max Ranseder of Postfach 11, Hydroanlagan, 4974 Ort im Innkreis, Austria, has designed two complete growing units, called the Maramatic Compacta and the Maramatic Electrona, which will serve varying numbers of containers in different rooms in buildings and homes, from a central tank. This control device can be installed in the basement or backyard and it passes new nutrient solution automatically through pipes to the troughs or pots as required. These hydroponic installations can be bought with full instructions for setting them up and are likely to become very popular for larger offices and households.

MUSHROOMS

Mushrooms are lower plants or fungi and differ from the green or higher plants in the way in which they feed. They cannot therefore be grown in standard hydroponic growing media or by using the normal nutrient solutions. In small-scale laboratory work, mushrooms may be cultured in agar-agar jelly with added sugars, or in treated sawdust with some added oatmeal. This method would be too costly and troublesome for the housewife or amateur gardener. However, because mushrooms are a popular domestic crop, a simple method of soilless cultivation has been devised for home use.

The easiest way to grow mushrooms at home is to raise the crop in shallow wood troughs filled with a simple growing medium. This method is particularly suitable for householders who may wish to produce moderate quantities for family consumption. The troughs can be kept without inconvenience inside rooms; in attics or cellars, or in garden sheds. By arranging the trays or troughs in tiers, or in series on shelves, it is possible to raise considerable quantities of mushrooms from comparatively small areas, while periodical sowings will ensure that a crop is available all the year round. Cheap growing troughs can be made from fruit boxes, of the kind used for packing peaches or grapes. The best dimensions are about three feet long by two feet wide by some six inches deep. Each box should be lined with polythene sheeting. A gap of a foot should be allowed between troughs in tiers. Normally a trough with a growing space of six square feet will yield about seven pounds of mushrooms from every harvest period. By nailing strips of wood to the ends of sets of boxes it is quite simple to erect inexpensive tiers of mushroom troughs, and a number of such devices would form a convenient unit, depending on the space available and the production desired.

Once the troughs have been prepared, the next task is to make the growing medium. This is done as follows:

Take three hundred pounds of straw, place it on a large polythene sheet or on a concrete backyard, and wet it thoroughly with water. Leave this for two days. Then mix together one hundred pounds of sawdust, thirty pounds of bran, and enough water to moisten them. Add nine pounds of ammonium sulphate, nine pounds of super-phosphate, and four pounds of urea fertiliser. Make sure that all the nutrient salts are absorbed and the whole lot is well mixed. Now combine the straw with the sawdust, bran, and fertilisers and pile the entire mixture into a heap about four feet long by three feet wide by some three feet high. Water well so that the material is quite wet, with some seepage from the bottom of the heap.

In two days, the temperature of the heap should rise to 140° F to 160° F. On the sixth day, turn the material for the first time, by removing one foot of the compost from the sides and top of the heap, breaking up the remainder, and replacing so that the outer parts now form the inside and the inner portions become the outside. This procedure allows gas exchange to occur. While turning, sprinkle ten pounds of calcium carbonate over the material. Apply more water, ensuring that no dry patches are left in the heap. The temperature will rise again to about 150° F. On the tenth day turn for the second time, and then on the thirteenth day give a further turn, sprinkling twelve-and-a-half pounds of gypsum powder (calcium sulphate) over the material. Reform the heap, as before, and make additional turns on the sixteenth and the nineteenth days. On the twentieth day, break down the heap, spreading it out on the polythene sheet or concrete and sprinkling half-a-pound of Lindane insecticide over the soilless compost to check any pests that may be present. The material should be dark-brown in colour, without any objectionable odour, and possessing ample moisture when pressed in the palm of the hand. This is the soilless growing medium and it is now ready for use. There will be enough to fill about a dozen troughs of the size already suggested for household use.

The soilless growing medium or substrate is placed in the troughs to a depth of some five inches and pressed down gently. If necessary,

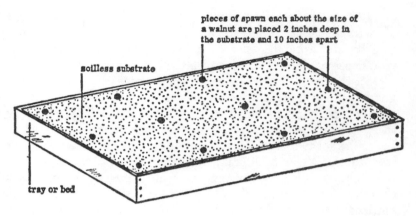

soilless substrate

pieces of spawn each about the size of a walnut are placed 2 inches deep in the substrate and 10 inches apart

tray or bed

Sowing the spawn.

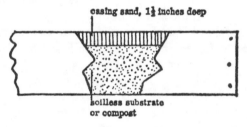

casing sand, 1½ inches deep

soilless substrate or compost

Side views of how mushroom trays or beds are arranged and grow.

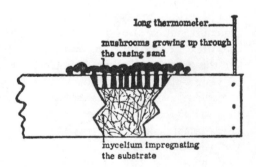

long thermometer

mushrooms growing up through the casing sand

mycelium impregnating the substrate

Fig. 21 The soilless compost is placed in trays or troughs to a depth of five inches and pressed down firmly. This leaves about an inch-and-a-half for applying the casing sand on top.

spray carefully with a little water to increase humidity. The temperature should rise to about 138° to 140° F. Maintain this heat for two days, then allow it to fall to 75° F by extra ventilation or inflow of fresh air.

Spawning may now be carried out. Pieces of spawn, each about the size of a walnut, should be inserted into holes two inches deep and ten inches apart in the growing medium. Grain spawn can be broadcast. The soilless compost around the pieces of spawn must be pressed firmly against them to give good contact or the mycelium will not spread well. Keep the temperature at from 70° to 75° F and certainly not below 65° F. Spray the troughs lightly with water daily. The mycelium will completely impregnate the growing medium or substrate in about two weeks, though occasionally it may take three. You will see the whitish thread-like growth permeating the soilless compost. As soon as this happens, the troughs should be covered with a layer of sand one-and-a-half inches deep. This job is called 'casing'. After casing, lower the temperature to 58° to 65° F, which is just right for mushroom production. Lightly spray the trays or boxes twice daily with water. The mushrooms should start appearing after fourteen days.

A good long thermometer is desirable for controlling mushroom growing. Keep a careful check on readings and use it regularly, inserting it right down into the growing medium. Mushrooms should be picked by twisting the roots gently, taking them out with the tops, disturbing the casing as little as possible. Any holes left should be filled immediately with fresh sand. Harvesting may last about two months. When bearing has finished, discard the old growing medium in the troughs or boxes and replace with a new lot. Careful watering helps to secure good yields. During cropping periods, it is normal to spray the troughs lightly with water to prevent the casing from becoming hard and dry. Light and frequent applications are best, rather than heavy ones at longer intervals. Good ventilation is important, to replace the fresh air used by the plants. Mushrooms exhale large amounts of carbon dioxide. Try to ventilate rooms and sheds for at least a quarter of an hour daily, but exclude any draughts. To keep troughs warm, it is practicable to use an electric heating cable or hot water pipes.

In mushroom growing with *this* soilless method, cleanliness is essential. Remove all stumps and pieces of stems left after picking. This prevents the growth of moulds on troughs. Weekly dustings with insecticide are helpful in keeping away pests like woodlice. Mushrooms have high food value and the flavour of home grown soilless garden ones is excellent, far better than stale shop bought lots. Also the cost of raising mushrooms at home is less than one-fifth of what you have to pay in greengrocers.

Here in condensed form is the formula for soilless growth of mushrooms.

Item	Quantity (in lbs)
Straw	300
Sawdust	100
Bran	30
Ammonium sulphate	9
Superphosphate	9
Urea fertiliser	4
Calcium carbonate	10
Gypsum powder (Calcium sulphate)	12½
Water as required	

Larger or smaller amounts may be prepared by multiplying or dividing throughout by a constant figure, keeping the relative proportions correct.

Schedule of Preparation of Growing Medium

DAY	TASK
1	Wet the straw
3	Add premixed sawdust, bran, ammonium sulphate, superphosphate, and urea. Stack into a heap. Water well
6	Turn for the first time. Add the calcium carbonate. Add more water
10	Turn for the second time
13	Turn for the third time. Add the gypsum powder
16	Turn for the fourth time
19	Turn for the fifth time
20	Break down the heap. Spread out on the polythene sheeting or concrete. Add insecticide. Material ready for use

CHAPTER X

Scope for Bigger Layouts

Once you have started a hydroponic home garden and become accustomed to the ease and simplicity of scilless plant growing using the simple method described in this book, you may well feel —if you have the space—that you would like to extend your unit. In the case of indoor pots and troughs this may be just a matter of multiplying the number of containers. However, where circumstances permit, other possibilities exist. For example, one can frequently lay out a small roof garden or use balconies and backyards or the edges of paths for interesting and profitable displays of hydroponics. Even in winter, it is quite simple to use polythene sheeting to erect cheap covers, plant houses, cloches, and similar shelters for tender plants outside the house. Glass-enclosed verandas protecting front doors or french windows also provide scope for tiers of attractively arranged containers. Of course, at cold times, it is necessary to fix up some form of heating, either by connection to the house installation or from electric heaters and paraffin stoves. Finally for those with a greenhouse or conservatory already available, conversion to hydroponics has numerous advantages. In hot regions, the merits of garden plant houses which afford shade and cooling sites are well known.

LARGER CONTAINERS

Usually, it is not recommended in bigger layouts that troughs should exceed three to four feet in width, otherwise attending to plants becomes difficult, but they can be of any convenient length, either straight or curved, according to individual taste. Normally, a depth of about six inches for most plants should be adhered to, except where special species are to be cultured. Some root vegetables, ornamental shrubs, and fruit trees like papayas or bananas, will need deeper containers. With larger troughs or beds, the drainage holes are generally placed at the sides, with a narrow guttering to carry away seepage. For ease of solution application and watering, a system of pipes or a prefabricated irrigation unit—there are several on the market, advertisements for which appear in the gardening and farming journals—or just a hose can be employed. Additional

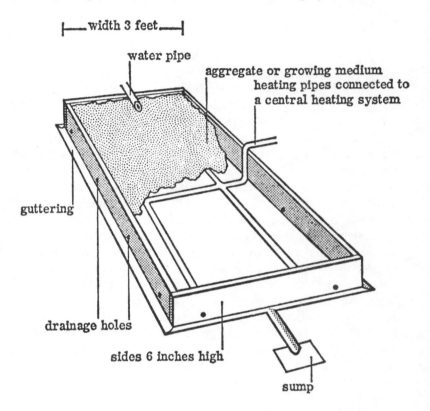

FIG. 22 A more elaborate hydroponic container. How heating may be laid on in bigger or more extensive hydroponic growing troughs.

refinements include automatic nutrient applicators, with time clocks, heating cables, and other apparatus. But here you are getting close to semi-commercial work, which is outside the scope of this present book. In Chapter XII some notes are given on various other methods of hydroponics and the reader may like to refer to some of the books and other literature listed below.*

* Pages 118–20.

SAVING MONEY

Have you ever calculated what you could save by growing your own vegetables in a home hydroponic garden, rather than collecting them in a basket or carrier bag from the local supermarket or greengrocer's shop? And what about the saving in time wasted trudging around the shops, to say nothing about the improvement in quality, taste, and food value you will have when you produce your needs in the house or backyard without any soil? A packet of seeds, for example, will cost only a few pence and can be multiplied into several hundred plants. Yet in the shops or market you will be asked ten or twenty times the price of these seeds for only just one stick of celery, a pitiful, stale and barely adequate lettuce, or a pound of tomatoes!

It is not necessary to have a large hydroponic unit to supply the main needs of an average household for fresh vegetables and salads. Even plots totalling no more than seven to ten yards long by some five yards wide will be a good basis to work on, expanding as you wish. Quite small indoor or kitchen units will provide a wealth of green salads. For community work, of course, bigger layouts will be wanted. In India, where household hydroponics is spreading amongst village and urban societies, it is considered that the simple method of hydroponics can supply eighteen hundred adult persons with a good meal of three pounds of greenfood daily throughout the year, from each acre of soilless garden under cultivation. This equals a yield of over eight hundred tons annually per acre. The vast potential of the system can be seen clearly from such results.

You can appreciate what hydroponics could mean to you and your family from the above performance. Especially in congested industrial cities and towns, the possibilities are great. The value of having your own source of fresh food inside the home is a real addition to personal income. Flowers, too, add beauty to our lives and help us to feel happy and cheerful.

Beginners anxious to extend their hydroponic units can think of investing in crops like herbs, including mint, thyme, sage, parsley and chives, which need very little attention, as well as regular crops of new potatoes. Plant the early varieties for speedy development. A few peas are also well worthwhile. The dwarf varieties can be grown without supports. French beans, too, will stand by themselves and are therefore easier to manage than runners.

The dwarf scarlet types grow only sixteen inches high and crop very early. Any surplus may be salted away for later use. Carrots, if properly looked after, beetroots, and onions, are very much appreciated. Start pulling the first carrots as soon as they are finger-size. Those not eaten at once may be packed away in very slightly moistened peatmoss for consumption in due course, if you like young and tender ones at different times. Celery is popular and much easier to grow in hydroponics than in soil, where the digging and earthing-up are laborious tasks. You can also get self-blanching varieties of celery, if you do not want to put collars of plastic on the ordinary kinds. Examples of these are Gold Self-blanching and Greensleeves. Brussels sprouts will repay a little effort. The Aristocrat is a variety with a cropping period of five winter months. It is also quite a small plant—an advantage where space is limited. The sprouts are tight and firm and have a delicious nutty flavour. Moreover, after all the sprouts have been harvested the stems will produce young tender shoots which make excellent spring greens. Purple-sprouting broccoli is very hardy and may be grown in outside troughs during winter time. The young tips make a delightful dish. Leeks are always acceptable. Salad crops such as lettuce, endive and radish should be exploited to full advantage, particularly as inter- and catch-plantings, with successional sowings to give a series of yields producing continual supplies of fresh home produce. These are only a few suggestions—you will no doubt be able to think of many more interesting and profitable arrangements for the soilless garden.

LAYOUTS

Convenient and well designed layouts for hydroponic gardens of bigger size will help householders and amateurs to work more efficiently and economically. Save yourself as much time and labour as possible. There is no hard manual work in soilless culture, but you can still look for improvements in the arrangements for maintenance. Good planning in advance brings better returns. If you are interested in expanding your hydroponic unit into a size-able installation for producing ample amounts of greenfood and flowers, perhaps surplus to your family needs, which you might sell part of, then organise it into the following sections.

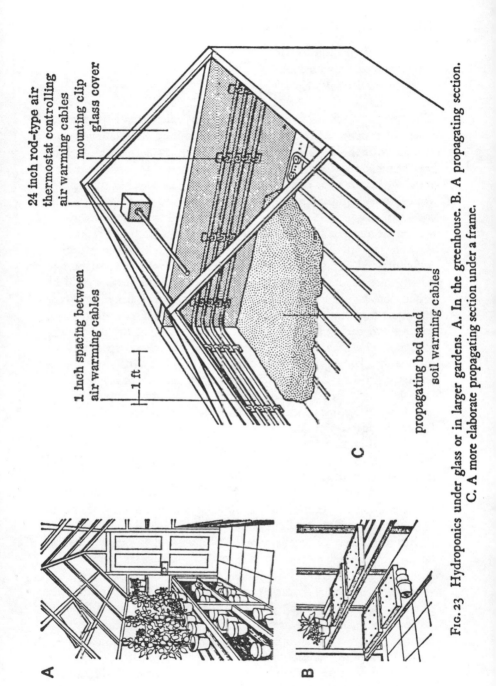

24 inch rod-type air
thermostat controlling
air warming cables
mounting clip
glass cover

1 inch spacing between
air warming cables

1 ft

propagating bed sand
soil warming cables

C

Fig. 23   Hydroponics under glass or in larger gardens. A. In the greenhouse. B. A propagating section.
C. A more elaborate propagating section under a frame.

(a) the propagation section
(b) the production section
(c) the service section

The propagation section is where you raise small plants for eventual transfer to the production department. The latter is concerned with the growing and output of the crops themselves. The service section includes the labour and facilities that keep the project moving, that is your own good right arm, plus possibly the help of your family, and the knowledge supplied by your learning. Also the tools that you use. As a general rule, the total area of the propagation section need not exceed three to four per cent of that of the production section. The propagation department should constitute a self-contained outfit situated near the main troughs or containers in a convenient spot. If possible, propagation boxes or trays should be raised above ground level. This saves much time because it avoids any need for kneeling or stooping during the routine operations of sowing and caring for seedlings and other tasks. In the production section, any number of containers may go to make up a unit or installation. In large-scale work, the United States Army used as its standard growing unit a set of ten troughs, each three hundred feet long by three feet wide. A ten-bed unit occupies approximately half-an-acre of ground, with paths and ancillary services and facilities. In greenhouses, troughs may be erected on existing staging or benches. Often five to ten beds are operated as one unit, with walks provided between the rows of troughs or containers. The Miami hydroponic gardens, in Florida, are based upon an original design of one hundred troughs, each a hundred feet long by three feet wide, with the nutrient solution flowing down a special flume to irrigate the growing medium in these containers. At the University of Reading's horticultural station at Shinfield in Berkshire, several large greenhouses were converted to hydroponics as long ago as 1946. In Tanzania, South Africa, and Rhodesia, open-air troughs are very practicable with shading provided by natural trees. In the hilly districts of north Bengal, terraced beds on mountain sides give satisfactory results. The first trials held at the Government experimental station at Kalimpong, near Darjeeling, depended upon gravity flow of the solution into the hydroponic beds.

When hydroponic garden units are started in hot tropical localities, it is best to site the troughs or containers on a north–south axis.

This facilitates the effective shading of plants with overhead mats or canopies from the scorching rays of the noonday sun. In temperate colder places, the best use should be made of available light. If strong winds are prevalent, the troughs or containers should be laid out, if possible, parallel to the direction of the wind. However, this need be no obstacle to hydroponic gardening—in Colorado growers have to contend with winds of one hundred miles an hour at certain times of the year, but suffer no serious ill effects. Economy of space should always be aimed for. The walks between individual troughs need not be more than three feet in width, just enough to admit barrows and other appliances for harvesting, if the size of the unit justifies their use.

Whatever shape of style of layout for larger installations is chosen, it should be tailored to fit the requirements of the house-holder or amateur gardener. Use your ingenuity to make your own designs and improvise as much as you can. To save expense employ whatever materials and equipment you may have on hand. Never waste money in buying costly devices and unnecessary apparatus. Any person can, with the exercise of a little imagination, design for him- or herself very satisfactory and attractive layouts for soilless gardening at home.

In bigger hydroponic units, it is just as well to have a shed for storing your fertilisers and other equipment. There you can keep your hosepipes, watering cans, spare containers, seeds, weighing scales, tools, and any other items you use, all tidy and in good order, ready to find just as you require them. Dry storage arrangements will be needed for fertilisers, insecticides, fungicides and suchlike. Also a table for the scales or balance and for writing your notes and records.

TESTING

As you become more advanced in working larger hydroponic units, you may like to do a little testing. Strictly speaking, these procedures are really designed for commercial operators engaged in large-scale production. However, you can quite easily check on the quality of your nutrient solution as it is absorbed by the hydroponic plants. Hydroponics experts regard the balance of the liquid plant food or its pH—that is the alkalinity or acidity of the solution—as a main factor in ensuring that flowers and vegetables grow well. To test the pH, you will require what is called an indicator. This can be bought or ordered from a good chemist. Ask for a Universal indicator. Having obtained a small bottle of indicator, you should proceed as follows.

About a quarter of an hour after irrigating or applying the nutrient solution to the growing medium in a hydroponic container, make a hole some four or five inches deep in the aggregate, near a plant. You should find some moisture at the bottom of this hole. Using a medicine dropper suck up a little of the liquid and put it on a clean white saucer. Before doing this, take care to wash the dropper in clean distilled water thoroughly and also put on clean well-washed rubber gloves. Now with another dropper, also washed in distilled water, take a tiny portion of the Universal indicator from its bottle and squeeze it into the solution you have taken from the growing medium. Watch the colour change carefully. If the result is a red or orange liquid in the saucer, the solution is too acid. A green or greenish-blue colour means that it is too alkaline. The right colour is yellow to yellow-green. That will give you a pH reaction of about neutral or in technical terms 6·0 to 6·5. Actually anything from about 5·0 to 7·0 is tolerable, but the most satisfactory reaction is in the region of 6·0.

Further information on testing procedure and how to control the pH reaction will be found in more advanced books on hydroponics. If you are using a proprietary formula or nutrient mixture you should get in touch with its manufacturer to ask for comments and advice.

CHAPTER XI

Helpful Notes

This chapter contains a variety of information which may be useful to beginners in soilless gardening, ranging from advice on different aspects of the system, weights and measures, list of books for further reading, and miscellaneous notes for housewives and amateurs.

HYDROPONICS AS A NATURAL SYSTEM OF PLANT GROWING

From time to time, you may hear criticisms that soilless cultivation is an unnatural way of nourishing and growing plants. Now, it is perfectly true that artificial fertilisers are often injurious in *soil* gardening and farming, because their use alone and unrestrictedly can destroy the land and eventually result in serious erosion. There-fore, in soil cultivation, mineral salts should always be applied in conjunction with organic manures. But in soilless gardening there is no soil to damage and therefore this criticism is in no way valid.

The growing media in which hydroponic plants thrive and develop is inert, durable, and not subject to erosion or destruction. As we know, plants derive the greater part of their food from the air, but they cannot exist without supplies of mineral elements and water. When growing in the earth, crops absorb these from the soil through their roots. Some of the mineral salts originate from the weathering of rock fragments, but nitrogen, one of the most important, is produced mainly from dead vegetation and animal remains. Of course, no organic manures can be directly absorbed by the roots of higher plants, but must first be broken down by bacterial action to ammonium compounds and finally to nitrates. Only then do they become of any value to the feeding of the plants. Thus when farmyard manure or compost are applied to the soil they have first to be converted in it to an 'artificial' fertiliser before they can become available for crop nourishment. Green plants can only take up inorganic salts in solution with water; they cannot 'eat' any organic matter or humus.

In hydroponics we simply give the mineral salts direct, no process of change has to occur, and consequently the needs of the plants are met immediately. There is nothing unusual about this, because chemical fertilisers are basically the products of normal and natural substances. Hydroponics is in no way unnatural—it simply cuts out an unnecesary part of the life cycle, avoiding the lengthy process needed to change a manure or organic material into an inorganic salt. Growth is also speeded up as each plant is assured of maximum sustenance at all times. The soilless method is simply quicker and better, under the right circumstances, than soil cultivation and a lot cleaner and easier too.

FOOD VALUES

The nutritional value of hydroponic vegetables and fruits is satisfactory. Analyses have shown that the mineral and vitamin contents are quite normal. In fact, it is possible to grow tomatoes containing extra calcium for feeding to babies and more iron for invalids. The same applies to other produce. Wheat raised in soilless gardens has been found to be better for bread making. Flavour of hydroponic greenstuff and fruits is excellent and the author has never found any person who was not impressed by the taste and quality of the produce from well-run soilless units.

WEIGHTS AND MEASURES

Most of the weights and measures in this book are given according to the Imperial system, because this will be most familiar to English-speaking readers. However, for those who wish to work with the metric system, here are the equivalents, as well as some other relevant information for reference.

Equivalents

1 ounce	28.35 grammes
1 pound	0.4536 kilogramme
1 gallon	4.546 litres
1 inch	2.54 centimetres
1 foot	30.48 centimetres
1 yard	0.914 metre

1 square foot	9.29 square decimetres
1 square yard	0.836 square metres (m²)
1 metre	3.280 feet or 1,094 yards
1 m²	10.763 sq. feet or 1,196 sq. yards

The litre was abolished in 1964 as a scientific unit of volume, but is still in common use. One litre = 1000 cubic centimetres (c.c.).

Metric System

10 grammes	1 decagramme
10 decagrammes	1 hectogramme
10 hectogrammes	1 kilogramme (kilo)
10 kilogrammes	1 myriagramme
100 myriagrammes	1 millier or tonne

Imperial System

12 inches	1 foot
3 feet	1 yard

Avoirdupois Weight

16 drams	1 ounce
16 ounces	1 pound
112 pounds	1 hundredweight (cwt)
20 hundredweights	1 ton (2240 pounds)
1 short ton	200 pounds

Surface Measure

144 square inches	1 square foot
9 square feet	1 square yard
4840 square yards	1 acre
43560 square feet	1 acre

Therometer Readings
Fahrenheit: Boiling 212° F, Freezing 32° F.
Celsius or Centigrade: Boiling 100° C, Freezing 0° C.

To reduce Fahrenheit to Centigrade, subtract 32 degrees and multiply by $\frac{5}{9}$; to reduce Centigrade to Fahrenheit, multiply by $\frac{9}{5}$ and add 32 degrees.

Note: The increasing use of metric weights and measures throughout the world makes it desirable that everyone should familiarise him- or herself with the system. The same applies to Celsius or Centigrade thermometer readings.

Fluid Measure

20 ounces	1 pint
8 pints	1 gallon

Capacity Measure

4 gills	1 pint
2 pints	1 quart
4 quarts	1 gallon

Cubic Measure

1728 cubic inches	1 cubic foot
27 cubic feet	1 cubic yard

Inches are divided into eighths, fourths (quarters) and halves, i.e., $\frac{1}{8}$, $\frac{1}{4}$ and $\frac{1}{2}$, $\frac{3}{8}$, $\frac{5}{8}$, and $\frac{7}{8}$, as well as $\frac{3}{4}$, are also quite common. 1 litre of water weighs 1 kilo. 1 gallon of water weighs 10 lb. 1 U.S. gallon equals $\frac{4}{5}$ of the Imperial gallon (approx.).

FURTHER READING

Here are some useful books that may be of value to readers interested in studying more about hydroponics. Unfortunately, however, most of them are no longer in print and copies will have to be borrowed from public libraries or can normally be loaned from agricultural and horticultural stations or University faculties of agriculture and horticulture.

General hydroponics

CULTURES SANS SOL by P. Chouard. La Maison Rustique, Paris.

HYDROPONICS AS A HOBBY. University of Illinois, College of Agriculture, Urbana.

HYDROPONICS: THE BENGAL SYSTEM by J. Sholto Douglas. Oxford University Press, Bombay and London.

HYDROPONICS—THE SCIENCE OF GROWING CROPS WITHOUT SOIL by Joseph P. Biebel. Florida Department of Agriculture, Tallahassee.

Nutriculture United States War Department Technical Manual.
U.S. Army Adjutant-General Publications Center, Saint Louis.

Profitable Growing Without Soil by H. F. Hollis. English
Universities Press, London.

Soilless Culture Simplified by A. Laurie. W. Heffer & Sons,
Cambridge.

Soilless Growth of Plants (Second Edition, revised by T. Eastwood). Reinhold Publishing Corporation, New York.

Successful Gardening Without Soil by C. E. Ticquet. C. A.
Pearson Ltd., London.

Water culture methods

L'Aquiculture by M. V. L. Homes, J. R. Ansiaux and G. Van
Schoor, Ministere des Colonies, Bruxelles.

The Complete Guide to Soilless Gardening by W. F. Gericke.
Prentice-Hall Inc., New York.

The Water Culture Method of Growing Plants Without Soil
by D. R. Hoagland and D. I. Arnon. University of California.

Tropical work

An Experiment in Soilless Cultivation. Information Directorate,
Government of Uttar Pradesh, Lucknow.

Practice of Soilless Cultivation (Sharder Process) by V. K.
Chatterjee. Alpha-Beta Publications, Calcutta.

Technical Publications

Lectures on the Inorganic Nutrition of Plants by D. R.
Hoagland. Chronica Botanica Co., Waltham, Mass.

Proceedings of Asamblea Internacional de Hidroponia, 1969,
Las Palmas. Published by the Secretariat of the International
Working-Group on Soilless Culture (I.W.O.S.C.) P.O. Box 52,
Wageningen, The Netherlands.

Sand and Water Culture Methods Used in the Study of Plant
Nutrition by E. J. Hewitt. Commonwealth Bureau of Horticultural
and Plantation Crops, East Malling, Kent.

Testing hydroponic nutrients

THE CHEMICAL TESTING OF PLANT NUTRIENT SOLUTIONS by G. S. Fawcett and R. H. Stoughton. The Tintometer Ltd., Salisbury.

Flower Growing

FLORICULTURE: FUNDAMENTALS AND PRACTICES, by A. Laurie and V. H. Ries, McGraw-Hill Book Co., Inc., New York.

FLOWERS AND VEGETABLES WITHOUT SOIL by A. J. Simpson. The London Gardens Society.

NUTRIENT CULTURE OF CARNATIONS IN SAND. British Carnation Society.

Vegetables

HYDROPONICS—CULTURE OF VEGETABLE CROPS by J. G. Stout and M. E. Marvel. Florida Agricultural Extension Service, Gainsville.

THE SOILLESS CULTIVATION OF VEGETABLES IN INDIA by J. Sholto Douglas. *World Crops* (Vol. 7, No. 2, 56–60, 1955. and SOILLESS CULTIVATION. *Nature* (Vol. 175, No. 4464, 884–5, 1955).

Fertilisers

COMMERCIAL FERTILIZERS, THEIR SOURCES AND USE by G. H. Collings. McGraw-Hill Publishing Co., Ltd., London.

TRACE ELEMENTS IN PLANTS by W. Stiles. Cambridge University Press.

LIST OF CONSULTANTS

The International Working-Group on Soilless Culture (IWOSC) maintains a register of consultants who have indicated their willingness to advise on hydroponics. The following list gives names and addresses as available in 1971.

Name	Address
R. M. Adamson	Research Station, Saanichton, Canadian Department of Agriculture, Saanichton, British Columbia, CANADA

A. Anstett

Ecole Nationale Supérieure
d'Horticulture,
4 Rue Hardy, Versailles,
FRANCE

A. R. Arredondo

Apt. Postal 1778,
Mexico, D.F.,
MEXICO

Atouq Al Bakheed

Hydroponic Section,
Ministry of Public Works,
Kuwait,
KUWAIT

Subhi Attar

P.O. Box 4424, Kuwait,
KUWAIT

A. Benvenuti

Istituto Agronomia Generale
e Coltivazioni Erbacee,
Via S. Michele degli Scalzi 4,
Pisa,
ITALY

D. Blanc

Station d'Agronomie Générale et
de Physiologie Végétale,
45 Boulevard du Cap,
06 Antibes,
FRANCE

C. Blesa

Universidad de la Laguna,
Tenerife, Canary Islands,
SPAIN

T. C. Broyer

Department of Plant Nutrition,
3044 Life Science Building,
Berkeley 4, California,
U.S.A.

R. P. Cairns

P.O. Box 763, Kitwe,
ZAMBIA

J. Cardua Aquilar

Estación de Floricultura,
Instituto Nacional de
Investigaciones Agrónomicas,
Barcelona,
SPAIN

V. K. Chatterjee	Hydroponic and Fish Investigation Unit, 45/4 Nilkamalkundu Lane, P.O. Sibpur, Howrah, West Bengal, INDIA
J. K. Choate	Pan-American Hydroponics Inc., P.O. Box 470, Grapevine, 76051, Texas, U.S.A.
Y. Coïc	Station Centrale de Physiologie Végétale, Etoile de Choissy, Route de St Cyr, 78 Versailles, FRANCE
G. S. Davtyan	Institute of Agrochemical Problems and Hydroponics, Armenian Academy of Sciences, Noragyugh 108, Erevan 48, U.S.S.R.
M. Deidda	Istituto di Agronomia Generale e Coltivazioni Erbacee dell' Universitá di Sassari, Via E. de Nicola, Sassari, Sardinia, ITALY
R. Favilli	Istituto di Agronomia Generale e Coltivazioni Erbacee, Via Michele degli Scalzi 4, Pisa, ITALY
E. Feiler	Kibbutz Yad Hanna, Mobile Post Lev Hasharon, ISRAEL

N. O. Fialho

Centro Brasileiro de Pesquizas Hidropônicas,
Travessa Meruípe 3 (V. Mariana)
São Paulo,
BRAZIL

T. Geissler

Institut für Gartenbau der Deutschen,
Akademie der Landwirtschafts-wissenschaften zu Berlin,
Groszbeeren,
EAST GERMANY

Z. Guminska

Ogród Botaniczny,
Uniwersytetu Wroclawskiego,
Wroclaw,
ul. Kanonia 6/8,
POLAND

J. J. Hanan

Department of Horticulture,
Fort Collins,
80521 Colorado,
U.S.A.

D. A. Harris

J. Muller Laboratories,
P.O. Box 2611, Capetown,
SOUTH AFRICA

E. Head

P.O. Box 386, Estancia,
87016 New Mexico,
U.S.A.

E. J. Hewitt

Horticultural Research Station,
Long Ashton, Bristol,
GREAT BRITAIN

Y. Hori

Laboratory of Physiology,
Horticultural Research Station,
1519 Nakahara-Shimojuku,
Hirtsuka, Kanagawa 254,
JAPAN

T. Ingestad

Royal College of Forestry,
Stockholm 50,
SWEDEN

A. Jungk

Institut für Pflanzenernahrung
der Technischen Hochschule,
Herrenhauserstrasze 2,
3 Hannover-Herrenhausen,
WEST GERMANY

Y. M. Khodjayants

Institute of Agrochemical
Problems and Hydroponics,
Armenian Academy of Sciences,
Noragyugh 108, Erevan 48,
U.S.S.R.

C. M. Lahora Arau

Jefatura Agronómica de Las
Palmas,
Calle Alfredo L. Jones 49,
Las Palmas de Gran Canaria,
Canary Islands,
SPAIN

C. Lesaint

Station Centrale de Physiologie
Végétale, Etoile de Choisy,
Route de St Cyr,
78 Versailles
FRANCE

E. Litton

Linda-Mar Cooperation,
P.O. Box 458, Makati,
Rizal,
PHILIPPINES

E. F. Maas

Research Station, Saanichton,
Canadian Department of
Agriculture,
Saanichton, British Columbia,
CANADA

J. Marcos

Istituto Forestal de
Investigaciones y Experiencias,
Carretera de Caruña K 7
Apt. 8–111
Madrid 20,
SPAIN

M. T. Marzo	Istituto Forestal de Investigaciones y Experiencias, Carretera de Caruña K 7 Apt. 8–111 Madrid 20, SPAIN
F. Massantini	Istituto di Agronomia Generale e Coltivazioni Erbacee, Via Michele degli Scalzi 4 Pisa, ITALY
Y. May Raz	Hydroponics Eilat, P.O. Box 189, Eilat, ISRAEL
H. Menon	Caixa Postal 5705, Sao Paulo (1) S.P., BRAZIL
G. Milletti	Istituto ed Orto Botanica della Universitá di Perugia, ITALY
J. Miranda de Onis	Instituto Nacional de Investigaciones Agronomicas, Madrid, SPAIN
J. T. Mullinex	Pan-American Hydroponics Inc., P.O. Box 470, Grapevine, 76051 Texas, U.S.A.
P. Olivera Criker	Avenida 3 de Mayo, Apt. 63, Santa Cruz de Tenerife, Canary Islands, SPAIN
E. Ortiz de la Tabla y Lopez	Jefatura Agronómica de Las Palmas, Calle Alfredo L. Jones 49, Las Palmas de Gran Canaria, Canary Islands, SPAIN

B. Padilla

Cultivos Especiales 'Llano Verde'
Granadilla de Abona,
El Medano, Tenerife,
Canary Islands,
SPAIN

J. Padila Godoy

Servicio Agrícola,
Domingo J. Navarro 5,
Las Palmas de Gran Canaria,
Canary Islands,
SPAIN

A. Panella

Istituto di Allevamento Vegetale,
Perugia,
ITALY

F. Penningsfeld

Institut für Bodenkude und
Planzenernährung,
Post- und Bahnstation,
8050 Freising,
WEST GERMANY

G. Perez Melian

Instituto Canario de Medecina
Regional Canalejas 39,
Las Palmas de Gran Canaria,
Canary Islands,
SPAIN

A. Pilgrim

Hydroculture Inc.
1516 North 7th Avenue,
Phoenix,
85007 Arizona,
U.S.A.

P. Pinucci

Via Targioni Tozzetti 32,
Florence,
ITALY

J. E. Quevedo Martinon

Santiago Rusinon 4,
Las Palmas de Gran Canaria,
Canary Islands,
SPAIN

M. R. Quintana Marquez	Lepanto 8, Las Palmas de Gran Canaria, Canary Islands, SPAIN
J. B. Rabie	P.O. Box 4628, Johannesburg, SOUTH AFRICA
M. Ranseder	Postfach 11, 4974 Ort im Innkreis, AUSTRIA
D. Reinhold	Institut für Gartenbau der Deutschen Akademie der Landwirtschaftswissenschaften zu Berlin, Groszbeeren, EAST GERMANY
F. Reyes Alzola	Venegas 1, Las Palmas de Gran Canaria, Canary Islands, SPAIN
S. Reynolds	South Pacific Regional College of Tropical Agriculture, Alafua, Apia, WESTERN SAMOA
J. W. S. Richmond	Whitehall Nursery, Whitehall Road, Peel, near Blackpool, GREAT BRITAIN
G. Rivoira	Istituto di Agronomia Generale e Coltivazioni Erbacee dell' Universitá di Sassari, Via E. de Nicola, Sassari, Sardinia, ITALY
J. Rodriguez Chicimo	Leon y Castillo 521, Las Palmas de Gran Canaris, Canary Islands, SPAIN

O. Ruthner	Sieveringstrasse 150, A-1190 Wien, AUSTRIA
M. Sachs	Volcani Institute of Agricultural Research, P.O. Box 6, Bet-Dagan, ISRAEL
M. Schwarz	Negev Institute for Arid Zone Research, P.O. Box 1025, Beersheva, ISRAEL
J. Sholto Douglas	Hydroponic Information Centre, P.O. Box, 31, Bombay, INDIA and c/o Ely House, 37 Dover Street, London W.1 GREAT BRITAIN
B. G. C. Smith	Gran'Anse Experimental Station, P.O. Box 166, Mahe, SEYCHELLES
J. V. Smith	Smith Hydroponic Seedlings, P.O. Box 227, Westoriana, Transvaal, SOUTH AFRICA
M. H. Soghigyan	Institute of Agrochemical Problems and Hydroponics, Armenian Academy of Sciences, Noragyugh 108, Erevan 48, U.S.S.R.
G. E. Staehelin-Stylen	Finca Los Mangales, c/o Enrique Escalente P. Salamá B.V., GUATEMALA
O. Steineck	Institut für Pflanzenbau und Pflanzenzuchtung, Hochschule für Bodenkultur, Wein, AUSTRIA

A. A. Steiner

Centrum voor Plantenfysiologisch
Onderzoek,
Postbus 52,
Wageningen,
THE NETHERLANDS

R. D. Stitchbury

Industrial and Hydroponics
Developments,
9 Nelson Street,
Marlborough,
NEW ZEALAND

J. L. Weihing

University of Nebraska,
Department of Plant Pathology,
East Campus, Lincoln,
68503 Nebraska,
U.S.A.

F. M. Yamaguchi

12727 Saratoga Creek Drive,
Saratoga,
95070 California,
U.S.A.

NEMATODES

Perhaps you have seen these small pests, also called eelworms, in garden soil or composts. Occasionally, they have been known to occur in hydroponic growing media due to outside infection very often caused by planting seedlings with old soil still around their roots—bought from shops or nurseries—in soilless garden containers. Nematodes can damage plants. These pests belong to many different strains and species. Probably the worst are the root-knot eelworms which make galls on the plants' roots and can cause death of crops. Eelworm attacks soon result in wilting and stunting of plants. It is quite easy to see the minute white or brownish spherical bodies of the nematodes in the aggregate and on the roots. One of the best ways of guarding against infection, if you are working with larger boxes or troughs, is to keep a few African marigolds growing at intervals in the hydroponic containers. The roots of these plants release a secretion which repels eelworms, so that they will not remain in the soilless beds. The leaves also give off a powerful odour. However, the effects of the marigolds will not harm your ordinary flowers and vegetables. This procedure is based on the principle of biological control, a system now finding many supporters in horticulture. It is cheaper, and frequently better, than using heavy doses of pesticides, though you can of course obtain products to clear serious infestations of nematodes.

SPROUTED GREENFOOD

If you like sprouts of beans and peas as green vegetables, you can use the method described on page 94 for growing them, under the heading 'Germination Nets'. Make one of these devices and scatter the bean or pea seeds over the netting. Cover with a piece of damp blotting paper or thin cloth for a few days until the seeds have begun to germinate. Then remove the covering and keep the unit in a warm place, but not in too direct light. After a week or two the tiny seedlings will develop into luscious sprouts with ample, tasty, green tops. You can pick them at whatever stage you like, just when the sprouts are the height that suits your culinary requirements. Such green sprouts go very well in salads, particularly at times when other produce is short.

SOILLESS COMPOST

These days there is much talk about soilless composts. Just what are these? A compost is a fertilising mixture, the word being derived from the Latin term *componere*, to put together. To make a compost for ordinary garden use we normally mix up some soil, organic matter, manures, and a 'starter' to activate the materials. In due course, these will heat up and mature into a compost. Now, a soilless compost, of course, contains no soil, being usually made from mixtures of sand and peatmoss, with some added fertilisers. It does not need any heating process. This material can be used to grow plants in for limited periods, but as soon as the nutrients in it are exhausted it has no further feeding value and the plants growing in it will gradually weaken and die. Soilless composts may be considered a part of gardening without soil, but they are not true hydroponics. For one thing they provide no permanent source of nourishment for plants. Then, they are frequently ill-balanced and gardeners cannot control the feeding of plants growing in containers filled with them. Such composts bear no comparison with the advantages of inert aggregates for maximum production. All the same, you may find a use for soilless composts from time to time for raising seedlings and occasionally for house plants or ring culture. Never add any manures or other dirty organic materials to your soilless composts. Use only sand and peat, with some added nutrients and remember their life is strictly limited to only a few weeks or months. Then you must throw your soilless compost away and replace it with a freshly made up one.

Here is a good formula for making soilless compost

Item	*Amount*
	BY VOLUME OR BULK
Fine sand	8 gallons
Peatmoss (preferably) sterilised with boiling water and clean)	8 gallons
	BY WEIGHT
Hoof and horn meal	4 ounces
Superphosphate	4 ounces
Ground chalk	4 ounces
Ground magnesium limestone	12 ounces
Potassium sulphate	½ ounce
Potassium nitrate	½ ounce

You can use an empty one-gallon petrol or oil can, with the top cut off, to measure out the sand and peatmoss. Mix them well together. Then weigh out the fertilisers separately on a kitchen scale or balance and mix them all together. Sprinkle the mixture over the sand and peatmoss that you have already mixed up. A further thorough mixing must then be done to produce a compost with all the ingredients evenly distributed throughout it. After placing the soilless compost in the pots or boxes, water carefully, so that it is just damp. Over-watering should be avoided or the plants may suffer from mildew and lack of aeration.

Note. The fertilisers mentioned above may be obtained from agricultural and horticultural merchants, at some big chemists, in shops of the general store type, garden centres and nurseries in many cases. If in difficulty, it may be useful to contact the local horticultural advisory service in your area.

CHAPTER XII

Using Other Methods

In this chapter brief descriptions are given of various other methods of hydroponics. The idea is to explain concisely how these function, so that the beginner, after having become familiar with soilless gardening by using the simple method described in the main parts of this book, may later go in for more elaborate techniques if he or she so desires. Not all of us want to indulge in what can be slightly ambitious projects, but there is no doubt that once you have been bitten by the hydroponic 'bug', you may well feel impelled to exploit the system to the full. There is something fascinating and very satisfying in utilising these resources of science and technology—today known as industrial biology—to produce better plants under closely controlled conditions. Even on a small scale in the home, backyard, or garden, you can employ quite elaborate methods of soilless cultivation to raise crops of striking quality by means of different apparatus and contrasting sets of equipment.

All methods of hydroponics conform to the same basic system. Soilless cultivation is a branch of horticulture, which draws upon agricultural chemistry, engineering, plant physiology and related sciences to achieve optimum results. For the sake of convenience, the different hydroponic methods or techniques may be classified under four main headings: *water or solution culture*; *sand culture*; *aggregate culture*; and *miscellaneous practices*. Each method contains within its limits a number of sub-divisions, generally intended to suit certain areas or purposes. The choice of a particular method normally depends on factors such as climate, place, availability of requisites, and costs. There is no 'best' method of hydroponics as such; what matters is whether the technique selected meets the requirements of those using it and the environmental circumstances.

The simple method that has been recommended for beginners in the preceding chapters of this book falls under the heading a mixed aggregate culture, combining the advantages, as well, of sand and solution culture. It is well suited for use in the home and can be operated by amateurs and housewives without difficulty. Moreover, no elaborate equipment is required, while results can be just as good as those secured in far more sophisticated methods. So don't rush to set up advanced and possibly costly installations, until you are sure you really want them or feel quite confident of handling them to full advantage.

Let us now discuss the different methods in turn.

WATER OR SOLUTION CULTURE

Plants of all kinds have been grown successfully in water or solution culture and the method has been employed for many years in laboratory tests. On a larger scale, it has given good results in commercial work.

The Standard Jar

This is quite easy to set up for home use, especially for the growth of ornamentals in individual containers. Any kind of glass or porcelain vessel may be employed, but the best receptacles are probably ordinary wide-mouthed fruit jars of one or two pints capacity. Flat corks, with a hole in them, or wads of non-absorbent cotton, should be fixed firmly in the necks to hold the plants in position. The roots are submerged in the nutrient solution, which fills the jar to within about two inches of its top, leaving a small space for air. Clear glass containers should be covered with dark paper to exclude light from the roots. To provide aeration, it is necessary to remove the plants from the jars every few days and then shake the solution vigorously or else to blow air into it with a bicycle pump or by mouth through a tube.

Continuous-flow

With this method, the solution is placed in a vessel attached to a small reservoir by a siphon tube. An outlet pipe, operating as another siphon, extends from a point near the bottom of the jar to a second overflow vessel, so creating a continuous flow of solution through the whole apparatus. By raising or lowering the end of the outlet, it is possible to vary the level of the nutrient solution around the plant's roots. At intervals, air is blown into the solution.

Drip

Virtually the same apparatus is used for the drip technique as for the continuous-flow arrangement. However, to avoid the need for blowing or pumping air into the solution a gap of about four inches is left between the end of the siphon tube which takes the nutrient solution from the reservoir to the container, and the funnels that receives it at the top of the container or jar. By careful adjustment of the siphon the solution can be made to drip out. Each drop collects some air as it crosses the space between the end of the tube and the funnel. This bubble of air is carried down into the region of the plant's roots, which grow in the solution in the vessel.

Swiss or Plantanova

Here we have an egg-shaped vessel. In its upper quarter there is a small detachable tray filled with stone chips resting on a wire grid. The root crown of the plant is supported on this grid, while the stem protrudes upwards into the air. Removable lids with a hole in them cover the tops of such vessels. The plant's roots descend through the mesh of the grid into the solution which is poured into the pot or vessel. Several sizes are available or can be made up quite simply.

Wicks

Cylindrical lamp wicks, as well as those made from glass wool, are used in hydroponics to irrigate the roots of plants growing on trays set above containers filled with solution. In this case, the roots do not normally descend down through the mesh into the liquid to obtain food, but instead the nutrient solution passes up the wick to the roots and so keeps them moist and nourished.

Gericke

This has developed from the original technique utilised by Dr Gericke in California. It has given excellent results under different conditions and is sometimes called tank culture. However, it may be a little difficult to handle for beginners living in damp localities. Nevertheless, the Gericke style of hydroponic units are being employed in Poland today for commercial production. Waterproof basins, troughs, or tanks are needed, to hold the nutrient solution. A wire grid fits over the top of each container and serves as a support for the plants, whose roots descend through the mesh into the liquid below. A covering of some material such as wood-wool, coarse peat-moss, shavings, or rough dry hay or any other form of litter, is placed on the grid. This excludes light from the nutrient solution in the container and provides additional support and protection for the crops. Aeration of the root system is ensured by adjusting the level of the solution, so as to leave an air space between its surface and the base of the wire grid. In certain units, air is blown through the liquid plant food from time to time, or extra ventilating holes are made in the sides of the troughs just above the solution surface and below the bottom of the wire grids. The last named is the technique adopted at Wroclaw University.

To operate a water or solution culture unit of the Gericke type the following information will be helpful.

The tank or container may be of any convenient size as long as it is easy to reach all parts. Waterproof materials are necessary for construction. The wire mesh framework should be supplied with

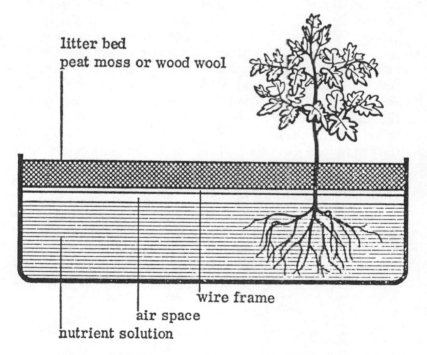

litter bed
peat moss or wood wool

wire frame

air space

nutrient solution

FIG. 24 A Gericke type unit for water or solution culture.

brackets or catches to keep it about two or three inches from the top of the tank. A low guard around it will serve to keep the litter in position. Whatever material you use to form this litter bed should be spread carefully over the grid and be of even composition and quite level. Sow the seeds on the litter and sprinkle a little extra material over them to supply some covering. Then moisten the litter with nutrient solution. Meanwhile, you will have poured enough solution into the tank below to reach up just to the bottom of the wire grid. This will ascend into the litter bed by capillary attraction and keep it constantly damp, as well as providing the source of permanent nourishment for the plants. If the material is allowed to dry out, the plants will, of course, die. Small seedlings can be set in the litter, if desired, with their roots positioned close to the top of the mesh. In time, these will grow downwards into the solution below. As soon as whatever plants you have selected are a few inches high you will find that their roots are passing through the grid and feeding on the liquid in the tank. When this happens, lower the level of the solution so that only about half of the length of the developing roots is immersed. The idea is to provide enough air for healthy growth. Continue to do this as the size of the roots increases. Remember that this aeration factor is very critical. Lack of air is indicated by a yellowing of the plants' leaves. It is necessary to keep the tanks covered with the grid and litter bed, but from time to time you can lift the tops off to inspect the roots and solution below. Blowing air into the solution occasionally helps. If holes have been provided in the sides of the containers, it is quite simple to glance through them to check the level or insert the tube of a bicycle pump there.

Once the tank has been filled with nutrient solution, you will need to top it up periodically with a little plain water and every fortnight empty it and refill with another batch of solution, freshly made up. Sometimes, the solution for water culture can be stronger than for mixed aggregate or sand methods. To prepare this, add up to fifty per cent more fertiliser salts to given quantities of water. Very much depends on the growth and appearance of the plants, which you will have to judge in the light of your experience.

SAND CULTURE

There are several variations of this method. In its simplest form, it resembles very much the technique of mixed aggregate culture already recommended in this book for beginners. However, sand culture, that is using sand alone as a growing medium, suffers from the drawback that it may be liable to waterlogging and retention of excess moisture in beds or containers. In practice, receptacles for sand culture need not be well waterproofed, and indeed beds or troughs can be laid down on any hard surface or sunk into the ground. This, of course, results in some loss of water and nutrients and greater ultimate costs.

Surface watering

Frequently termed the slop technique, here we have plants grown in improvised beds or receptacles containing sand only, the solution being applied by can, pipe, or irrigation system to the surface of the material. Free drainage is permitted. Surface watering is very easy to operate, but, as already stated, it is wasteful of water and nutrients. In addition it can be very messy in the home.

New Jersey

Essentially, the New Jersey techniques involve the use of an elevated tank from which the nutrient solution flows by gravity into the troughs filled with sand. Alternatively, it may be pumped several times a day to give similar results. In household work, hydroponic window boxes with a sand growing medium can be fitted with rubber squeeze bulbs and check valves, so making periodic manual irrigation possible. Another way is to spray the nutrient solution over the surface of the containers or pots in the soilless garden. In the Middle West of the United States, large scale hydroponics operated by automatic solution flow into sand beds is known as the Withrow technique.

Automatic Dilution Surface Watering

A concentrated solution is diluted to the required strength and then applied to the sand-filled troughs or containers by means of a system of sprays. This was employed at Jealott's Hill Research Station, operated by Imperial Chemical Industries Ltd. A low pressure water-main is needed, in addition to an injection pump and reservoir. To secure improved drainage, a layer of small gravel can be placed at the bottom of the containers underneath the sand.

Wick

A double pot arrangement is used. The upper receptacle consists of an ordinary flower pot filled with coarse sand and fitted with a glass wool wick, which passes through the bottom hole into the lower container. This second vessel is watertight and holds the nutrient solution. The wick, which is divided at the top and branches out to facilitate adequate distribution of the solution in the root zone, draws up the liquid plant food from the lower to the upper pot.

Drip

Using a feed line or thin tube, diluted nutrient solution contained in a tank elevated above the level of the plants' growing receptacles, is allowed to drip continuously on to the sand medium. The nutrient solution percolates through the sand, is collected in another tank, and pumped back to the original tank or reservoir at intervals. For drip techniques, a waterproof container is necessary.

Continous-flow

The hydroponic container should be placed on a stand, under which is kept a basin or bowl to receive any seepage or drainage. From a nearby tank, a siphon and feed pipe maintain a continuous flow of nutrient solution onto the surface of the sand in the trough or pot. This technique is quite handy for household use.

Modified Slop

This arrangement was developed by Dr F. M. Eaton of the United States Department of Agriculture. The nutrient solution is pumped through devices which flood the surface of the sand beds or troughs, at regular intervals. It then percolates down through the growing medium and eventually drains back into an underground tank for storage. The technique may not be very suitable for salad crops, such as lettuce, which do not tolerate large amounts of free liquid around their root crowns.

Dry Application

Here, instead of dissolving the fertiliser salts in water to form a nutrient solution for application to plants, the formula is sprinkled dry on the surface of the sand in the hydroponic containers. As soon as this has been done, the mixture is washed down into the root zone with a spray of plain water or by using a can or hosepipe. This makes it go into solution beneath the surface of the growing medium. Stated amounts of formula are applied dry to given areas of space, normally about an ounce to each square yard weekly or fortnightly. Dry application is a very simple manner of working a hydroponic unit, provided you remember to sprinkle the fertiliser mixture carefully and evenly, and water it well in. Failure to stick to the quantities laid down, and the procedure, correctly, can cause serious injury to plants. It has given excellent results in many regions, particularly in household soilless gardening.

For all sand cultures, good aeration is vital. Seeds may be sown directly into the growing medium, or young seedlings planted in small holes made in it. Many hydroponicists use trays of sand to raise stock for later transplanting into the main containers in the soilless garden. Sand culture is also excellent for rooting cuttings, while bulbs thrive in it, if well aerated. Remember always that over-irrigation is dangerous and care must be taken to watch this point. In the home, perhaps the simplest way to employ sand culture is to stand pots full of sand, the bottoms of which have a layer of broken bricks, cinders, or pebbles placed in them, on saucers or shallow trays. These will catch any seepage. Pour the nutrient solution gently on the surface of the growing medium in the containers and keep the sand constantly moist.

AGGREGATE CULTURE

Numerous different growing media can be used in aggregate culture. These include gravel, broken-up bricks, washed cinders, clinkers, stone chips, leca, pebbles, vermiculite, and other substances of inert nature. Mixtures of two or more are also practicable. Aggregate culture is much employed in commercial hydroponics in all parts of the world. All the same, despite its complications, the scientifically minded beginner can quite easily construct smaller soilless gardens, using a technique of semi-automatic aggregate culture in the home or amateur garden.

Sub-irrigation

Watertight troughs or containers are necessary, and these are filled with gravel or some other hard inert medium. The beds must be flooded periodically with nutrient solution and then allowed to drain. For irrigation, direct-feed and gravity-feed apparatus may be satisfactory. Sometimes, cascade troughs or tanks are built, so that the solution flows from one to the next before discharging. Troughs or beds may be built of any suitable materials. A reservoir, a sump, and a pump will be required. The entire technique is automatic, and by virtue of the ebb and flow of the nutrient solution the roots of the plants are well aerated. Sub-irrigation is a very economical way of feeding crops. There should be no loss of water and nutrients. In addition, the grower has complete control over the plants. On the other hand, the apparatus can be expensive to install and the units rather complicated to construct. Nevertheless, in large scale commercial soilless gardens, money is saved on labour and maintenance.

Flume

This device consists of a long, curved, artificial channel down which the nutrient solution is directed, so that each trough or bed may receive a correct proportion of the liquid as the flush sweeps by. Flumes are employed in commercial hydroponics, particularly in Florida.

Bucket and Gravity Feed

Usually a small trough is constructed about three feet above ground level, with a taller post secured to the rear for hooking a bucket on to, or if a larger unit is contemplated, then with an overhead rail to which a series of buckets may be attached. A hose is joined at one end to the bottom of the bucket and at the other to the base of the side-wall of the trough containing the growing medium. When the bucket has been filled with the nutrient solution and raised to the elevated position, the liquid plant food flows down into the trough or bed, irrigating the roots. By dropping the bucket to the ground level, drainage of the growing medium is accomplished by the outward and backward flow of the solution. This method is quite convenient for householders, but needs frequent attention.

Compressed Air Design

The nutrient solution is contained in large drums, placed at ground level. From these it is driven into the troughs or beds by portable air compressors. Drainage is by normal gravity flow. This technique has been used in the West Indies and in the Middle West States of America.

Wick Devices

These can be utilised in small aggregate cultures and are quite valuable for seedling propagation work. Basins containing the nutrient solution are located underneath the troughs filled with gravel or other growing media, which are kept moist by the capillary action of the wicks. These run from the basins up into the aggregate through holes in the bases of the troughs. They are fitted so as to draw a constant supply of nutrient solution from the basins to the growing media.

Bengal

This technique was developed originally at the Government of West Bengal's experimental station near Darjeeling in India, and has given excellent results subsequently in many other countries. Troughs or containers made from any suitable material are used. These are filled with a fairly coarse aggregate, made up of a mixture of gravel or stone chips and sand. The nutrient formulae are

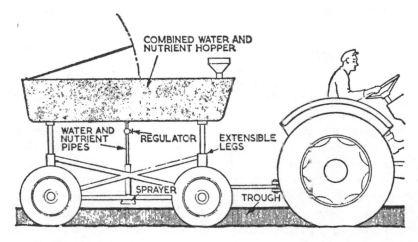

FIG. 25 Hydroponics—the Bengal System. Tractor and spreader designed for applying nutrients in large hydroponic units. The machinery travels along the troughs quite quickly. The plant food is spread on the surface of the aggregate and is washed down to the roots with water from the tank or hopper.

applied, normally in the dry state, to the troughs and then immediately watered into solution with sprays or hosepipes. By sprinkling the fertiliser salts evenly between the rows of plants, good distribution of the nutrients is assured. Normal irrigation facilities are provided through systems of pipes in large units. The aggregate in the containers must be kept constantly moist. In big installations, machinery is used for spreading the formula. The technique is simple to maintain, easy to operate, and cheap to install. It is also adaptable to widely contrasting conditions, and can be very useful for amateur gardeners and householders as well as for commercial production.

Vermiculite Technique

When vermiculite aggregate is employed in hydroponics, care has to be taken that its water holding properties do not give rise to an excess of moisture in the containers. Vermiculite may retain supplies of available water or solution for hydroponic plant growth for up to ten times as long as some other aggregates do. It is very light and easy to transport. In general, there are advantages in mixing vermiculite with sand or finer media. It is not always recommended for sub-irrigation work, but does very well in slop or other cultures.

Aggregate Hydroponic Units for the Home

Here are some suggestions for operating a small aggregate hydroponic unit in the home or backyard.

A waterproof container must be used. Plastic, enamel or other troughs are quite suitable, but if a metal receptacle is chosen, be sure to paint it first with good quality varnish or paint, but not tar. You can aim to provide a supply of nutrient solution through a hole or aperture in the bottom of the trough or container for the plants in such a way as to ensure that all the aggregate inside is well and thoroughly moistened. To achieve this, lay a small perforated pipe or rose in the bottom of the container, connecting this to the hole. A hose fitting should be fixed in the hole, so that the pipe or rose can be attached to it on the inside. At the same time, this will enable you to fix a further piece of piping to the outside of the container. This pipe, in turn, should be connected to a bucket or tank, also having an aperture at its base, with a similar hose fitting in it. To feed the plants, fill the vessel with nutrient solution and site it

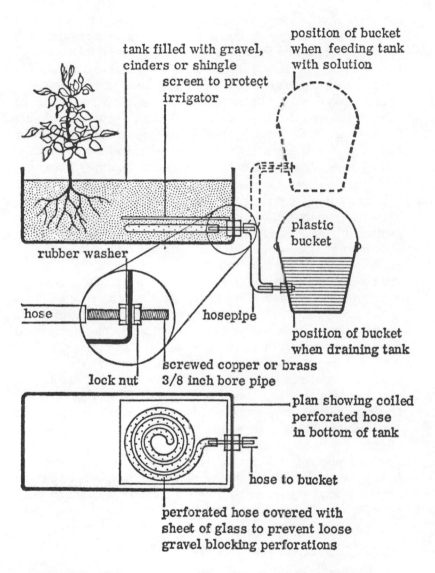

position of bucket
when feeding tank
with solution

tank filled with gravel,
cinders or shingle
screen to protect
irrigator

plastic
bucket

rubber washer

hose

hosepipe

position of bucket
when draining tank

lock nut   screwed copper or brass
3/8 inch bore pipe

plan showing coiled
perforated hose
in bottom of tank

hose to bucket

perforated hose covered with
sheet of glass to prevent loose
gravel blocking perforations

FIG. 26 Design for small hydroponic unit in the home or backyard.

above the growth container. The solution flows down into the aggregate by gravity, gradually permeating all the growing medium. To drain it off, change the position of the vessel or bucket to a lower situation, so that the liquid plant food runs out of the trough or container back into the vessel. Alternatively, you can have a fixed tank and feed by gravity, allowing the solution later to drain off into a sump, then pumping it back again into the elevated reservoir or storage tank. Feeding with nutrient solution is best done early in the morning, so that it can remain in the trough or container during the daytime. In the evening, start the drainage process, permitting this to go on all night. The cycle can be repeated continuously, adding fresh solution to the tank or bucket as required. The object is to keep the growing medium damp and fit for plant development.

In preparing a container for aggregate culture, using this sub-irrigation technique, take care to ensure that you make the growing medium of small pebbles, washed cinders, gravel, or other clean inert material. Do not use fine sand or ashes. The perforated pipe or rose at the bottom of the container should be laid flat on the base and covered with a sheet of glass, plastic, or other similar material, to prevent the aggregate being washed out through the perforations in the pipe. It must, in fact, be screened from the material inside the container. The perforated pipe or rose can be made of copper, plastic, or rubber, with holes about one-eighth of an inch in diameter, pierced into it at short intervals, so that the nutrient solution can flow freely, but not too quickly, out of the pipe into the growth container. The container should be at least six inches deep, to allow ample root space. It is better to coil the pipe in the bottom of the container to get more even distribution of the nutrient solution. Deeper containers or troughs may be needed for some plants. Standard nutrient solutions can be employed for plant feeding. In larger units, hydroponicists may find it worthwhile to invest in a small electrical pump connected to a time switch, which automatically supplies the container with solution at regular intervals.

MISCELLANEOUS PRACTICES

Many other hydroponic techniques have been utilised from time to time in different areas with success. Some of these have already been mentioned in this book, including germination nets, hanging baskets, tiers, and floating rafts (pages 94, 97 and 98). Then, there is *aeroponics* or the mist spray technique, where plants are grown in hollow tubes, with apertures for the stems and foliage to extrude. A very fine spray or mist of nutrient solution is passed along inside the tubes to supply the roots with water and vital nourishment.

Botuliform devices, or large plastic sausage-shaped containers filled with liquid plant food, are employed to grow algae for

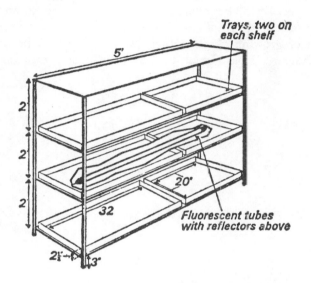

FIG. 27 A tier arrangement for hydroponics inside rooms or for growing different crops with added light. Designs can be varied in size to suit individual needs.

processing into edible and finished products for animal and human consumption.

Ring culture is a partial form of hydroponics, the plants being raised in pots or containers filled with soilless compost and standing on beds of moderately coarse and watered aggregate, into which their roots descend through the holes in the bottom of the pots.

Many more such arrangements are likely to be developed as the years pass. Indeed any gardener or householder with a mechanical or scientific turn of mind can easily adapt or modify existing techniques to suit his or her own convenience or situation. There is ample scope for improvisation and individual ingenuity in soilless gardening, provided you stick to the basic rules.

NOTE

Further information about different and more advanced methods of hydroponics may be obtained by reading some or all of the books and publications listed in chapter XI (pages 118–20). In addition, the Secretariat of the International Working-Group on Soilless Culture (IWOSC), P.O. Box 52, Wagingen, The Netherlands, has issued a comprehensive bibliography on hydroponics. The author will be happy to reply to enquiries from readers for further advice on any aspect of growing plants without soil. Letters may be addressed: c/o Pelham Books Ltd., 52 Bedford Square, London W.C.1, England.

Index